GOLF'S MISSING LINKS™

STEALTHY WAYS TO IMPROVE YOUR GOLF GAME

Dennis C. Sweeney, Ph.D.
Matthew J. Kluck,
PGA Master Professional

First Edition 2012

Sweeney, D. C. and Kluck, M. J. Golf's Missing Links: 101 Stealthy Ways to Improve Your Golf Game

ISBN: 978-0-9850214-0-5

© 2012 by Dennis C. Sweeney and Matthew Kluck, Inc. All rights reserved. Printed in the United States of America. Except as permitted under the United States Copyright Act of 1976, no part of this book may be reproduced or distributed in any form or any means, or stored in a database or retrieval system without the prior written permission of the publisher and authors.

Published by 101 Games for Golf.

Contents

A Word from the Authors VII

Acknowledgements IX

1 The Game Within the Game 1

The Game Within the Game

Seven Reasons This Series Is Unique

This Booklet Series Will Help YOU!

Meeting Your Expectations

How Golf's Missing Links Series Is Organized

Get Started!

2 Introduction to the Games: Who Should Play Them? 11

Golf Games: Stealth Learning

Skill Levels

Should I Play the Games Alone or With Others?

3 The Games 17

How the Game Chapters Are Organized

The Game Booklets

What You Need to Play the Games

Game Etiquette and Safety

4 The Short Game: Putting, Chipping, and Pitching 23

Putting Games: Flat Stick Magic

Introduction

Tech Talk: Choosing a Putter

Putting Game Booklet

A. Putting ON the Green (13 Games)

B. Putting FROM OFF the Green (4 Games)

Chipping: The Scoring Game

Introduction: The Chip

Tech Talk: Chipping

Your Go-To Club

Short Chipping Games
(1–15 yards)

A. Short Chipping (16 Games)

B. Long Chips and Recovery Shots (5 Games)

Pitching: Up and Away

Introduction: Pitch Shots

When Should I Pitch?

Tech Talk: Pitching

A. Short Pitches (5–20 yards)
(14 Games)

B. Long Pitching (15–50 yards)
(5 Games)

5 Full Swing: Tee and Approach Shots 51

Full Swing: Off the Tee

Introduction: The Tee Shot

Tech Talk: Off the Tee

Full Swing: Off the Tee (7 Games)

Full Swing: Approach Shots

Introduction: Getting to the Green

Length Does Not Always Matter

Tech Talk: Approach Shots

Reality Check: How Long Should I Be?

Swing: Approach Shots (10 Games)

6 Bunker Time 67

Introduction: Mastering the Bunker Shot

Tech Talk: Bunker Shots

What Kind of Club Should I Use?

A. Greenside Bunker Games
(12 Games)

B. Fairway Bunker Games
(3 Games)

7 Take It to the Course 75

Introduction: Take It to the Course

Tech Talk: Playing on the Course

On the Course (18 Games)

8 Turning Your Game Around 83

Rethinking Your Game

9 Evaluating Your Swing: Finding the Squeaky Wheel 87

Identifying the Squeaky Wheel: What Do You Need to Fix?

Self-Evaluations at the Range

Putting Circle

Swing Inventory: Short Chips

Chipping Circle

Swing Inventory: Long Chips

Swing Inventory: Pitching

Full Swing Inventory: Driving and Approach Shots

Greenside Bunker Evaluation

Swing Inventory: On the Course

Basic Shot Tracking

Advanced Shot Tracking

Thorough Shot Tracking

10 Goal-Setting: What I Want to Get—How to Know if I'm Getting There 105

Why Did You Buy This Book?

Home on the Range?

Goals and Expectations

Eat the Elephant One Bite at a Time

11 Learning How to Change Your Game 115

Introduction: How We Learn

Skill Learning and Muscle Memory

Tech Talk: The Learning Process

Learning Strategies

"I rebuilt my swing. My shots are better, but my scores are worse!"

If It's Bent or Broke, How to Fix It

Group vs. Individual Instruction

What to Look for in a Golf Teacher

12 Perfecting Your Practice 131

Introduction: Effective Practice Technique

Tech Talk: The Perfect Swing

The Role of Aids, Tips, Drills, Practice, and Games

The Practice Process

How to Practice for Improvement

When Should I Practice?

Practice for the Expert Player

13 Getting Ready to Hit: The Pre-Shot Routine 145

Introduction: The Pre-Shot

Why Is the Pre-Shot Routine Important?

Developing Your Pre-Shot Routine

Tech Talk: Psychology of the Pre-Shot Routine

Putting it Together

Pre-Shot Routine Sequence

The Role of Physical Rehearsal

14 The Mental Game: Mind Over Swing 157

Managing Our Emotions

Positive vs. Negative Thinking

Tech Talk: Where Your Negative Emotions Come From

Embarrassment

Stress

So What Are Your Golf Stressors?

Frustration and Anger

Keeping Your Perspective

See You on the Course!

Appendix 185

A Word from the Authors

In 2008, I (Dennis) was asked to help Tiger Hubbard, an excellent junior golfer, with some problems in his short game. Tiger had a competent instructor, but found routine practice sessions tedious and boring.

To make these practice sessions more entertaining, I developed a chipping game we called *Swamp Monster*. This simple game required Tiger to chip over a towel, which represented the swamp, to a target on the green. To make it more interesting, we made it a chipping competition that Tiger could play in his back yard with his friends.

Later I showed Tiger another game, *Putting in the Dark*, where he had to putt to a target with his eyes closed.

Tiger's dad felt that these two games helped his son improve his game, and his subsequent awards as a junior golfer in western Pennsylvania supported his observation. Based on this positive response, I approached Matt, and the idea for this book was born.

Golf's Missing Links is the result of over two years of work. Matt and I brainstormed the games and he would try them out with his students. This was a perfect fit since Matt had more than 200 active clients and had recently become the coach of our local high school girls' golf team.

Before Matt's tenure, this team had never won a match since 2009 and was dangerously short of players. Under his tutelage, the girls improved their average team score by more than 25 strokes per match and won five matches. They are now thriving with a full complement of players.

Golf's Missing Links does not champion any specific golf method or technique. Instead, it helps you master the method you are most comfortable with **by giving you dozens of games, ranging from putting and chipping competitions through tee and bunker play.** There are even games to be played on the course. Each of these games helps you practice more effectively while enjoying the time you spend on the practice green and range.

We also have chapters that focus on how to learn and practice effectively. These are based on time-tested learning techniques developed over decades of applied psychological research.

This series is for you if you can answer "yes" to any of these questions:

- Have you ever felt you mastered some golfing technique during a lesson only to find that it deserted you on the course?
- Have you spent hours on a practice tee and felt that you were wasting your time?
- Have you ever said to yourself, *"Why can't I play as well as I practice?"*
- Have you ever had difficulty telling your golfing teacher what problems you were having?
- Have you ever wondered what a pre-shot routine was and how to develop one for yourself?
- Have you ever wanted to develop a systematic practice routine?
- Have you ever wanted some entertaining games to play with a child or companion that did not involve time on the course?
- Are you motivated to learn and want to develop your game on your own?

If you follow our simple practice advice and suggestions, you will not only practice more *efficiently*—you will practice more *effectively*. You will learn how to develop a goal for each practice session and an efficient practice plan.

There is a well-known saying that applies to people who feel their game is limited by their equipment, no matter how well they play: "The problem is not with the nail, it is with the carpenter." This series is dedicated to all of you carpenters out there who want to enhance your golf games. We hope you enjoy it as much as we enjoyed creating it!

—Dennis and Matt

Acknowledgements

We gratefully acknowledge our colleagues and friends, who helped us craft this book together:

- George, Barbara, and Tiger Hubbard
- Merrilyn Gibbs, Coach of the California University of Pennsylvania Woman's Golf team
- Dr. Vanessa McKinnon, LPGA Professor at California University of Pennsylvania Professional Golf Management Program
- Justin Barroner, Chair, California University of Pennsylvania Professional Golf Management Program
- Our design team – Shawn Atkins, Fred Schroyer, and Jim Scattaregia
- Dr. Karen Bush, colleague and friend
- Peter Coughlin, Coach of the California University of Pennsylvania Mens' Golf Team
- Erin Zeddies
- Our advisory group – Jim Cichra, Gordon Vietmeier, Scott Koontz, and Kevin Shields
- Michele Berteotti, LPGA
- Mark Martens, USGTF Certified Teaching Professional
- Golf, the wonderful game itself
- And of course our wives, Janet Kluck and Martha Sweeney

The Game Within the Game

Matt Kluck, a PGA Master Professional, has been teaching golf for more than 25 years. A student suggested that he write a golf instruction book. Matt replied, "that's impossible. I'd have to write a book for each of my students, since each has a slightly different swing. Since no one swing fits all golfers, I'd have to write more than two hundred books!"

(Famous last words. Here's the book!)

Reading this book and playing the games will help you to:

- Boost your skill at envisioning and making shots—on, around, and away from the green.
- Enhance your feel for the game of golf without boring, repetitive drills.
- Understand how you learn to play the game of golf.
- Discover the areas of your golf game that need to be developed.
- Develop an efficient practice routine tailored to your personal goals.
- Document your progress both on and off the course.
- Expand your understanding of what each club can and cannot do— on, around, and away from the green.
- Build your confidence in go-to shots and clubs.
- Develop your personal pre-shot routine.
- Identify and overcome mental roadblocks that can hurt your game.
- Most importantly, **have fun** while improving your golf game!

The Game Within the Game

Fredrick Nietzsche, the great German philosopher, wrote, *"You have your way. I have my way. As for the right way, the correct way, and the only way, it does not exist."*

Fred probably wasn't a golfer, but his statement, like Matt's comment to his student, applies to golf. There is no one perfect swing that applies to all players, but there are good and bad ways to learn the swing that is best for you. That is what this book is about. It is about learning your golf swing and having fun while doing it.

Learning Through Games

While most golf instruction books focus on mechanics or the mental aspects of the game, this one does neither *and* both. The series *Golf's Missing Links* is really about how to enhance your golf skills by playing what we call **The Game Within the Game**. As you can see, we have a pretty ambitious goal for you: helping you to become a better, more confident golfer while having fun in the process.

We show you new ways to improve your swing through a wide series of games you can play, either alone or with other golfers. This is learning while having fun—**stealth learning.** We tell you about good and bad learning strategies, how to identify your golfing strengths and weaknesses, and how to communicate these to your teacher.

Then we show you how to integrate your instructor's recommendations into an effective, personalized practice routine. To do this, we describe how you can practice more efficiently by giving you the vital link between (a) the stroke you felt you had grooved in a lesson or on the practice range and (b) playing on the course.

All golfers judge their performance in terms of the number of strokes it takes to complete a round of golf. Unfortunately, just counting swings at the ball does not help you identify what is working and what is not.

If one of your goals is to play better golf, we show you both simple and advanced techniques to identify your game elements that are strengths, and those you need to develop. To do so, we include detailed self-assessments to help you track your progress as your game improves.

Self-Evaluation and Personal Improvement

To become a more confident golfer, it is important to know which elements of your game you need to develop, and how to develop them. This book contains numerous self-evaluations that will help you to identify strengths and weaknesses you may have. They cover all elements of golf, from putting to driving. Using these assessments, we then show you how you can set realistic, personalized improvement goals and practice plans and how to implement them.

We will also guide you through the elements of an effective, personalized pre-shot routine. Finally, we will discuss some of the mental aspects of the game—the thoughts that get in the way of an effective swing, and those that help with a confident swing.

Our Objectives

While we have a number of goals, we really have three key objectives:

1. Show you how to play the **Game Within the Game**, games that are designed to strengthen your ability to play more consistently while having fun developing your swing.

2. Show you how to identify the **specific elements of your golf game that need to be developed** by giving you a wide variety of self-evaluation exercises to help you identify your golfing strengths and those elements that need to be enhanced.

3. Show you how to **Practice for Improvement** by helping you identify your practice flaws and design a personalized, efficient practice routine that includes our games.

Seven Reasons This Series Is Unique . . .

Dozens of learning methods and hundreds of golfing books focus on technique or the mental game. Some are pretty good. We are not biased toward any specific philosophy or technique—only on *enhancing your game*. With so much competition from superstars, what do we have to offer?

1. **We make practice entertaining.** Books, articles, and lessons often include drills using swing aids—sticks, socks, metal brackets, harnesses, and assorted medieval torture devices. Sometimes we get entranced by the latest learning gadgets—a hinged driver, magical perfect swing secrets, fuzzy tees, nuclear golf balls, or a seven-foot licorice-coated driver with a sweet spot larger than Rhode Island. But the simple fact is that none of these will be helpful unless they help you develop a swing that becomes integrated into your golf game through practice, and **practice can be boring.**

   > The more I practice the luckier I get.
   >
   > —Gary Player

   Most practice does not duplicate either the companionship of a sociable eighteen holes with friends, or the pressure of competition found in a tournament. This is one reason why your great shot on the practice tee doesn't show up on the course. To help you make the shift from practice to play, **our games integrate friendly competition with the skill development** you get through physical rehearsal and shot-making.

2. **We get you to *play* in situations that promote skill development in an environment as close to the course as we can make it.** Most practice sessions are done off the course, and this is true with most of our games. What makes our approach unique is that our games develop the skills used in everyday golf shots **with the element of competition**. We give you the opportunity to use what you learned in traditional lessons in a fun atmosphere. (We also show you the games that can be played alone as a form of "golf solitaire" when no playing companion is available.)

3. **We make learning fun.** Remember, golf is a *game*. It is supremely challenging, but it is still a game—and games are for enjoyment. Drills are not fun; they are work. Drills can, and should, help you learn a basic element of a successful swing. But drills alone will not help you develop your game. They must be integrated into your full swing. **Our games put drills into realistic action.**

4. **We help you understand what *all* your clubs will do—on, around, and away from the green.** It's important to develop a feel for a "go-to club"—one in which you have confidence. But better players experiment with a variety of clubs in varied situations to develop a feel for what each can and cannot do. Putting with a driver may feel weird, but playing one of our putting games with it will give you a sense that it can do more than smack a ball off the tee.

5. **The games can be played by players at all levels, *beginner to expert*.** The simpler games give you needed experience without the inevitable frustration that comes with acquiring basic swing mechanics. We have many friendly competitions that can be played by golfers of all ages. For example, it is **fun** for the accomplished player to play our easy game *Putting in the Dark* (see Putting booklet) with a learner. In contrast, it is challenging to play on-the-course games like *Adoption* or *Quarantine* found in the *On the Course* booklet.

> Golf is not a game of great shots. It's a game of the most misses. The people who win make the smallest mistakes.
>
> —Gene Littler

In fact, the easier games can be enjoyed by everyone. This is a great bonus for the parent who wants to have fun with a child or for couples of differing ability levels who want to play together. Two people can play any of the basic games without skill-level differences getting in the way of having a good time.

6. **We give you solid advice so you can Practice for Improvement.** Most golfing practice and range sessions can be categorized as either exercise or warm-ups. In our later chapters, we give you clear ideas about the psychology of skill-learning—and how you can use these ideas to develop specific goals and practice routines that achieve what most range sessions don't—help you groove an automatic, repeatable golf swing.

7. **Finally, we give you a structured way to track your development.** In fact, we encourage you to develop personalized golfing goals. If you are using this book to develop your game, it is

important to know what has to be fixed, and then develop a plan to fix it. In Chapter 10, *Goal Setting*, we tell you how to do it.

This Booklet Series Will Help YOU!

This book and its companion booklets will help *you,* regardless of your golfing level: *beginner* to *expert*, child or adult, teacher or learner, player or companion — any of the following . . .

Beginner, Occasional, Skilled, or Expert Player

No matter where you fit, **our games will improve your game**—enjoyably, intelligently, productively, efficiently. In Chapter 2, we discuss these four playing levels in detail and how our games can help them.

Junior Players

Learning golf is fun! Many of our games have been **"fun-tested" with junior players.** And we have taken their suggestions on how to make them even more interesting. No matter how good you are at golf, these games will make practice around the green, on the range, and even on the course more exciting.

Weekend Golfers

Weekend golfers are not always free to spend the time they want to practice. They just want to play. While regular practice is prerequisite to game improvement, this book can help you in other ways. For example, our suggestions for developing a pre-shot routine will help you become more consistent in your ball striking.
And many of our simpler games can be integrated into your pre-game warm up.

Parents

Parents want to have fun with their kids while their children learn golf, and vice versa. Many of our games are simple competitions that can **involve a parent who is helping a child** to learn golf. Even if the parent is not a *skilled* player, playing simple games is fun and develops a lifetime bond. (For example, check out two games in the Chipping booklet: *Between the Rails* or the chipping game *Swamp Monster* or *In the Pits*.

People Taking Lessons

Golf teachers expect you to practice what you've been taught. When you complete a golf lesson, you'll have ideas for the swing changes you need to practice. In Chapter 11, *Learning How to Change Your Game,* we explain the psychological principles behind real skill learning and what your teacher should discuss at the end of each lesson to help you integrate your learning into your swing. Then Chapter 12, *Perfecting Your Practice*, explains **how to make most effective use of your practice time.**

Teachers, Coaches, and Instructors

- **Junior golfers** in group instruction need constant activity to keep them occupied. Give them games to play in small groups to engage them productively while you instruct others. Most games can be played as small group competitions. Check out an easy chipping game, *Beginning Line Line-'em-Up* in the Chipping booklet, or a fun pitching competition, *Pitching Leapfrog* in the pitching booklet.
- For your students who get **overly anxious** under pressure these games can provide low-level competition. Use the games to help them to acclimate to a real game situation.
- To **help a serious golfers** who want to improve their games see Chapter 10, *Goal Setting*, for ideas on tracking their progress. Also, see the **diagnostic exercises** in Chapter 9**.** These can help you determine specific shots they need to develop.
- After each lesson consider each of our games **as homework** assignments to help your students acquire the specific skill set you are working on.
- If you are unfamiliar with the psychology of **skill learning** and how it relates to effective teaching, see Chapter 11, *Learning How to Change Your Game*. Chapter 12, *Perfecting Your Practice,* describes practice techniques to help both teachers and students.

Companions

We frequently see a spouse, girlfriend, or boyfriend take up golf to bond with their significant other who has more golfing skill. Unfortunately, it can frustrate both partners. The more experienced player may lack the inclination and patience to shepherd a novice for 18 holes, and the novice may become frustrated or bored with a game he or she may not understand.

Playing these games **gives couples a chance to share in the sport** without the pressure of playing the course. Since the basic games focus on elementary skills, the novice can play them without becoming frustrated and giving up. And the experienced partner just keeps getting better. These games are a win-win for relationships!

Meeting Your Expectations

To have real enjoyment in golf, you should have honest hopes about yourself and your game. Unmet expectations lead to frustration, and we certainly don't want you to be frustrated with us!

About the Book . . .

As we have said, we wrote this to give you ideas about how to **have fun on and off the course while enhancing your golf game**. It is not a book on technique. If you need to cure a hook or reduce the number of three-putts, then see a qualified teaching professional. We give some ideas in Chapter 11 on what to look for in a teacher.

The games will help you integrate your teacher's suggestions into your golf swing and make the process enjoyable. Your instructor should even recommend the games that will help you learn golfing skills quickly.

About Yourself . . .

You expect to become another Bobby Jones, Lorena Ochoa, Arnold Palmer, Ben Hogan, or Tiger Woods? Well, maybe you will, but unless you have the time, talent, and motivation of these superstars, it is more likely that you'll win the Powerball jackpot.

Having realistic expectations about what you can accomplish with your golf game is essential to both enjoying the game and the speed in which you will develop your golfing ability.

Most serious golfers would love to have the mental toughness of Suzanne Petterson, the steely determination of Tom Watson, the short game of Phil Mickelson, and the booming drives of Bubba Watson. Unless you happen to be one of those big names reading this book, IT AIN'T GONNA HAPPEN!

You should aim to be the best *you*, not the clone of someone else. Your goal is to develop the best game for you. We cannot emphasize this strongly enough!

How Golf's Missing Links Series Is Organized

Golf's Missing Links is a series of eight booklets that are integrated yet independent. It includes this basic book, six games booklets, and a *Practice and Performance Diary.* Here is a description of each.

This Book summarizes the games and how to play them. It is divided into two major sections:

Games Chapters:

2. This chapter identifies the different playing levels of golfers who can benefit from the games.
3. Here we overview the games and how to play them.
4. Introduces three short game booklets: putting, chipping, and pitching.
5. Reviews the full swing booklet: fairway shots and hitting from the tee.
6. Discusses the bunker play games.
7. Introduces the games that can be played on the course.

Learning, Practice, and Performance Chapters—*cover other aspects of improving your game:*

- **8.** Turning your game around.
- **9.** How to diagnose your swing strengths and weaknesses.
- **10.** Focuses on goal-setting.
- **11.** Shows how to learn most efficiently.
- **12.** Developing an effective practice technique.
- **13.** Developing a personalized pre-shot routine.
- **14.** The (important!) mental game.

The Games Booklets. There is a games booklet for each of the basic golfing swings: putting, pitching, chipping, full swing, bunker play, and on-the-course play. Each of these booklets contains from 15 to 21 games for players at all levels.

The Practice and Performance Log. This booklet helps you keep a record of your practice sessions, assess your swing development needs, and collect information about your on-the-course strengths and weaknesses. It is the perfect companion to this whole series.

Get Started!

If you want to . . .

- **Start having fun and developing your game,** go to Chapter 3 and learn about the games.
- **Diagnose your swing development needs,** do the self-assessments outlined in Chapter 9.
- **Prioritize your game development needs,** read Chapter 10.
- **Understand to enhance your learning and how to pick a teacher,** see Chapter 11.
- **Learn how to practice more efficiently,** read Chapter 12.
- **Develop an effective pre-shot routine,** go to Chapter 13.
- **Understand the emotional elements of golf,** read Chapter 14.

Introduction to the Games: Who Should Play Them?

On the Golf Channel, a well-known golf instructor observed that most people take lessons several times a year. Most of the time, they want to learn how to smash a drive and hit long irons. They rarely look for greenside shot advice, especially putting. We think this is strange. Golf scores are affected more by the short game shots than any other element of the game. Why not spend more time on them?

Reading this chapter will help you to:

- Understand your playing level so you can select games best-suited to your ability.

Golf Games: Stealth Learning

Obviously, the only way to learn golf is to practice the skills your teacher or coach recommends. You do not learn a skill by watching it or reading about it. You learn it by performing it and doing it often.

However, if we wrote a book titled *How to Practice Golf,* it would become the loneliest book in the store. *Our games are really stealth practice sessions designed to make learning an automatic swing enjoyable.*

Skill Levels

This book is for anyone who wants to play better golf. Since effective learning and practice varies with your playing ability, here are the four primary skill levels from *beginner* to *expert*.

1. Beginning Players

Who You Are:

- You are just starting to learn the game, and lack basic expertise and familiarity with golf.
- You get frustrated because you "*don't know what you don't know*" about the golf stroke. You just know your swing isn't working, the ball is misbehaving, and you don't know why.
- Your best learning strategy is to start simply and build on the basics.
- You learn best by listening to, observing, and imitating expert, qualified teachers. This includes watching instructors demonstrate basic elements of the golf swing and then attempting to repeat them.

As a beginner, you are *unconsciously not skilled*. This is not an insult—you don't know what you don't know! Your golf knowledge is not broad enough to play the game successfully.

To learn the swing, it must be broken into basic elements, with each element learned and practiced independently and then integrated into the full swing.

Before you can hope to hit the ball well you must learn the fundamentals of a proper golf shot: grip, balance, swing, and body movement.

You develop best through competent instruction followed by initial drills. You can improve quickly if you break your practice into small increments and avoid trying to overpower the swing in a marathon session. Later, these drills can be integrated into your full swing.

Beginners can become discouraged and frustrated if pressed too hard to take your games to the course.

We recommend:

- **Since our easy golf games** are tailored for *beginning* players, you can play them to learn simple swing elements quickly. The games help you get a feel for the basic golf swing and put into practice your teacher's suggestions. The first two or three games in each chapter are designed with you in mind—try them out!

- **Ask your teacher** to help you choose games that can help your basic swing.
- **Read Chapter 11,** *Learning How to Change Your Game.* It includes a section on what to look for in a teacher if you want professional help in enhancing your golf skills.
- If you want to **have fun learning without the pressure of hitting well on the course,** start with the putting games. This is one of the simplest strokes in golf—one that can give rewarding results immediately.

2. Occasional Players

Who You Are:

- You know you're not skilled but understand the basic golf swing and know what you need to learn.
- Your game frequently needs attention and focus on mechanics.
- Your poor shots often happen when you have too many swing thoughts or your swing thoughts are wrong. This creates confusion and lack of confidence.
- You learn best by performing the full golf stroke during and after instruction. This is the "Show Me/Tell Me How/Try It Out" stage of learning.

As the occasional player, you are aware of how much there is to learn, so you are *consciously not skilled*. You, unlike the *beginner*, know what you don't know.

You have developed a simple swing, but your game skills are basic and your stroke is often inconsistent. You can become discouraged because you make mistakes and don't know how to fix them.

Players at your level may drop out of golf because of frustration, impatience, and/or too-high playing expectations. Any of our games can help you to reduce this frustration.

You learn best through basic repetition and plenty of positive feedback. You can benefit from both our **easy and intermediate *games.***

We recommend:

- Prioritize the golf elements you want to develop, either by doing one of the self-assessment exercises in Chapter 9, *Evaluating Your Swing: Finding the Squeaky Wheel,* or in our *Practice and Performance Diary.*
- Self-evaluation gives you a baseline for **measuring your progress**. It also gives your teacher valuable information about areas of your game that need the most attention. Most students first meet their teacher with sparse information about their golf games. These assessments help bridge the information gap.
- To develop consistency, confidence, and skill, read and implement our recommendations for getting the most out of your practice time.
- Start developing your pre-shot routine. We tell you how in Chapter 13.
- In the meantime, try some of our **Easy and Moderate Games**—and have fun!

3. Skilled Players

Who You Are:

- You are confident in most elements of your game.
- You are familiar with a variety of shots off the tee and through the green.
- You hit the ball well, but inconsistency hurts your score.
- Your mistakes come from poor shot selection, unequal proficiency with all clubs, or limited chances to practice and play.
- You can improve quickly with little need to focus on basic elements of the swing since your major game improvement is usually limited by one or two basic flaws.

As a *skilled* player, you don't have to think about the basic swing—it has become automatic. You are *consciously skilled.* You are aware of what you do well and what you need to develop. You play often enough to enjoy golf without too much focus on mechanics.

We recommend:

- Playing all of the games in this book, because they help you get comfortable with every club in your bag. By playing our games you will learn shots you may not have considered in a conventional round.
- If you want to **enhance your skills** you can learn a lot from our games. Many can be played alone. They help you identify swing flaws and reinforce swing changes.
- As a serious player, you should complete the self-assessment exercises in Chapter 9, *Evaluating Your Swing*, and read Chapter 12, *Perfecting Your Practice*, to get the most from this book.

4. Expert Players

Who You Are:

- You play most shots automatically without thought.
- Your weaknesses may show up in one area of the game, but you mostly play most shots well.
- At the tournament level, you can develop and perform unique shots on the course. These creative trouble shots you rarely practiced.
- You automatically perform all elements of the game from ball striking through game and course management.

As a top-level golfer, you are the *expert*. You are *unconsciously skilled*. You have mastered most if not all of the aspects of the game, and you can visualize and execute shots without thought.

We recommend:

- **Try using our games to polish your game** and to pass on your knowledge and skills to less-accomplished golfers.
- **Play our games for the fun of it.** The moderate and advanced games are interesting ways to **add variety to your game and practice.**
- **Try some of the advanced chipping games and pitching games.** They focus on skills that can shave an extra stroke or two off your scores.

- **For fun,** look at some of the games in the booklet *On the Course.*

Should I Play the Games Alone or With Others?

The games can be played either as skill-building competitions or as individual solitaire exercises. When played alone, we recommend that you build them into your regular practice routine and select games that will help you develop your confidence in specific swing skills. You can also integrate some of them into your pre-game warm-up.

When playing alone, one way to get the competitive feel is to use several balls and pretend they represent different competing players.

3
The Games

Reading this Chapter will help you to:

- Discover how to get the most fun from our games.
- Understand how each of the games chapters is organized.
- Understand what you will find in each of the game booklets.
- Familiarize yourself with the elements of golfing etiquette as they apply to playing our games.

How the Game Chapters Are Organized

Each of the games chapters in this book contains these parts:

Introduction—Comments on the shot being made.

Tech Talk—Technical observations about equipment and the shots required for games in the booklet.

Game Summary—Presents a table summarizing each game. We review the game, its difficulty level, the players it will help, and a graph that indicates how well the it strengthens each of the following swing elements:

Visualization—Anticipating the ball flight before you swing.

Control—Managing the club face, swing path, and your body to make the shot you have visualized.

Confidence—Believing that you can make the shot you have visualized.

Versatility—Getting the same result using a variety of clubs.

Swing Feel—Developing your swing mechanics.

Here is an example from *On the Course*. This summarizes a game many of you know: *Best Ball Scramble*. The number preceding the game's name is its sequence in the book. In this case *Best Ball Scramble* is the first game in the *On the Course* booklet.

1 Best Ball Scramble	Easy			
Each player hits from group's best shot off the tee. • This low-key game reduces the pressure of having to hit a successful tee shot. • It lowers the pressure when you play with better golfers. Each player hits from the group's best shot off the tee.	Visualization			
	Control			
	Confidence			
	Versatility			
	Swing Feel			

H (for Home)—Some games can be practiced in your back yard if you have sufficient room and understanding neighbors! These are marked with an **H**.

The Game Booklets

The booklets offer a variety of games for golfers at all skill levels. Here is a summary of what you will find in each one.

Short Game Booklets

Putting: Flat Stick Magic (17 games)—13 games for putting on the green and 4 for putting from off the green.

Chipping: The Scoring Game (21 games)—16 games for hitting 1–15 yards from the green and 5 games for developing skill when faced with long chips and getting out of trouble off the green.

Pitching: Up and Away (19 games)—14 games for those short, tricky lofted shots you face when close to the green, and 5 games for longer pitches.

Full Swing: Approach and Tee Shot Booklet

Full Swing Shots (17 Games)—this booklet is divided into two sections. The first section has 7 simple tee shot games. Since you must tee-off on every hole these games help you with this inevitable shot. The second section offers 10 games for the full swing from the fairway. They focus on developing a feel for distance and accuracy.

Bunker Shot Booklet

Greenside and Fairway Bunkers (15 games) — Part 1 (12 games) focuses on greenside bunker shots, and Part 2 (3 games) focuses on fairway bunker shots.

On the Course Booklet

On the Course (18 games) — there are some standard games here like *Best Shot Scramble*, but we also provide 16 new competitions to help you transfer what you have learned in your practice sessions to the course. These games will help you develop confidence in hitting a quality golf shot, learn how to lower your score, recover from difficult situations, and think and play creatively.

What You Need to Play the Games

Play the games with the same clubs, balls, markers, and tees you would normally take to the course. A couple of them can be enhanced with some common household items:

Hula Hoops — make good targets for short pitching games at a practice range or in your backyard.

Paper Plates — make good targets to sharpen short game shots.

Small plastic laundry baskets — good targets, especially for chipping and pitching games (or use a cardboard box, range ball basket, or waste basket).

Rope tied in a circle — a target for longer shots. It takes a surprisingly long piece of rope to make a target, as the following table shows. For example, a 5-foot rope makes a pretty small circle, only 1.6 feet in diameter.

Circle Diameter (ft)	Rope Length (ft)
1.6	5
3.2	10
4.8	15
6.4	20
8.0	25
9.5	30
11.1	35
12.7	40
14.3	45
15.9	50

Other—For games where you chip over obstacles, you can use chairs or golf bags.

Game Etiquette and Safety

Important: Keep golf etiquette in mind while playing these games. Many involve playing on or around the green. Most likely this will be a practice green. You might even play some of them on the course.

Considerate golfers always keep the following in mind:

- **Get permission** from range managers if you place targets on or around putting greens or at a driving range. Be sure the retrieve them when you leave.
- **Don't disfigure or harm the playing surface of a green**. A green is one of the most difficult playing surfaces to maintain. Leave it smoother than you found it by leveling all pitch and spike marks.
- **Rake the sand smooth** if you're playing in a sand bunker, removing any pitch and shoe marks when finished. Leave it smoother than you found it.
- **Clean up after yourself**. It is annoying to find a tee box littered with dozens of broken tees. If you are playing games on the practice range, respect others—pick up and discard pieces of tees.

- **Be aware of where you are hitting the ball** if you are playing any of these games on the course or practice green. Stop play if there is a chance of hitting another player.
- **Be considerate of other players** using the green, bunkers, or range. You are sharing it with them—it does not belong to you. When playing these games, give plenty of space and playing room for others.
- **Don't hog green time**. Putting greens are one of the most popular places on the course. Other players use them for warming up before a round or as part of their practice routine. Be considerate and give them space.
- **Don't hold up groups behind you** if you are playing one of these games on the course.

Now you are ready for the games. Have fun!

P.S. If you have been counting you will notice that the games booklets really have 107 games, not 101. We thought that 101 sounded cooler than 107, and we wanted to give you more than you expected.

The Short Game: Putting, Chipping, and Pitching

Reading this chapter will help you to:

- Understand that mastering the short game can dramatically improve your score.
- Learn about key technical aspects of the short game.
- Learn about the variety of games we have developed to enhance putting, chipping, and pitching.

This chapter covers the three skill shots you need to score low when playing golf: putting, chipping, and pitching. Any accomplished golfer will tell you that mastering these shots is essential. There are games for players at all skill levels. If you do nothing else, we recommend that you devote at least half of your practice time to these games—whether you are playing them competitively or for individual self-development.

Putting Games: Flat Stick Magic

Mel was a skilled golfer playing in a competitive foursome with three friends. But for the past two weeks, Mel's putting had become more and more erratic. After fourteen holes, one of his friends commented on his troubles—and suggested that Mel try putting with his eyes closed.

His first putt, 4 yards, hit the center of the hole. Mel tried putting the same way for the next two holes and single-putted. On the 18th hole, Mel had a 40-foot breaking putt! Confident in the eyes-closed technique, Mel did it again for a birdie.

> **Putt:** a stroke where the ball stays on the ground with the goal of getting it into the hole.

Reading this section and playing the games in the Putting booklet will help you to:
- Understand why it's important to be fitted for a putter.
- Learn about the putting games in the putting game booklet to instill a feel for the basic putting stroke using:
    - A putter on the green.
    - A putter off the green.
    - Different clubs off the green.
- Reduce your tension over basic putts.

Introduction

Which club do you use most frequently during a normal golf round? Unless you are fantastically lucky, you would answer *"putter."* This club is used on every green. It can be either the "round savior" or the "round killer." In this chapter we focus on developing confidence in your basic putting game.

Tech Talk: Choosing a Putter

There is no substitute for technique when making any golf shot. While marketing executives want you to feel that the latest club with the most advanced exotic alloy will turn anyone into an instant scratch golfer, this is nonsense.

For the most part it is not the club, but *the golfer* that controls the ball.

On the other hand, poor equipment can limit you, especially if you use clubs that are incompatible with your build and swing style. This is particularly true for putters.

There is an endless variety of putters: mallet putters, blade putters, short putters, belly putters, on and on. No other club has such variety. So here are some ideas for putters . . .

> Real golfers don't cry when lining up their fourth putt.
> —Anonymous

What to Look for in a Putter

If you are seriously interested in getting the best-fitting putter, we recommend visiting a professional clubfitter. There are many good ones. Two independent organizations train and certify them: The Association of Golf Clubfitting Professionals (AGCP) and the International Clubmakers Guild (ICG).

Choosing a certified clubfitter ensures that you are in the hands of a specialist. Your PGA professional can also give you advice on fitting clubs to your stance and build.

On the other hand, if you don't want to go to that expense, here are three tips for getting the right putter:

- **Length**—this is the most important feature in a putter. Most standard commercial putters are designed for the typical golfer and are 33–35 inches long. Newer belly and chest putters are longer, but still come in relatively few lengths. While off-the-shelf sizes may work for the average person, the length may not be ideal for your preferred putting stance or stroke. You should never have to adjust your stance to fit any club—especially the putter.
- **Lie angle**—lie angle is a technical term for the angle of the putter shaft to the putter head. When you are ready to putt, the putter blade should be parallel to the green. This promotes clean putts and minimizes the risk of the club's heel or toe scraping the ground.
- **Weight**—weight focuses on the putter head. Weight should match the putter's length, shaft stiffness, and your personal style.

All three aspects can be corrected by a golf professional with the proper equipment. When testing and being fitted for a putter, always do so from your *address position*. Again, do not adjust your swing to the putter; the putter should be fit to accommodate your swing.

How to Repair a Pitch Mark (Ball Mark) on the Green

Few things are more annoying to golfers than to find pitch marks scattered like mini-meteor strikes on a green. (Pitch marks are depressions made in the putting surface by a ball when it lands on the green.) Failure to repair them is one of the more common breaches of golfing etiquette.

To make this repair properly, you need a repair tool similar to the one shown here. These are inexpensive mini-forks that help you move the small mound of earth found at the back of the pitch mark into the depression made when the ball makes an indent in the green. In a pinch, you can use a tee to repair pitch marks. But it is a poor substitute for this inexpensive metal or plastic repair tool.

More **importantly**, not all golfers know how to properly repair pitch marks. If you insert the tool under the pitch mark and pry up, you rip the grass roots, killing grass in and around the pitch mark. This leaves a brown dead spot that takes many days to regrow.

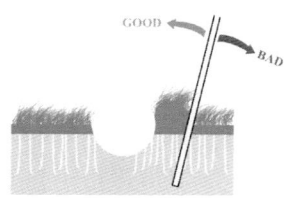

The proper technique for pitch mark repair is shown in this picture. Place the tool prongs at the edge of the ball mark and **lever the mound of dirt forward into the depression**, using a gentle twisting motion. This does minimal damage to the grass. Finally, tamp down any unevenness with the sole of your putter. Taking a few seconds to do this leaves the green surface smooth for the next players, an important courtesy.

Putting Game Booklet

The putting booklet has 17 putting games. The first 13 are played on the green, and the last 4 from off the green. We begin with very simple ones to give you a feel for distance and line and then progress to more advanced competitions. These games can be played by 2–4 players or more.

Most can even be played alone, in which case you can use several balls with each representing a team. When playing competitively, we suggest marking the balls for easy identification.

Please note: If you play these games alone it is important to move to a variety of positions rather than putting consistently from the same location.

A. Putting ON the Green (13 Games)

PUTTING ON THE GREEN GAMES	EVALUATION				
1 Putting in the Dark (On Green)	**Easy**				
Putt to a marker or a hole with your eyes shut. • This helps you develop distance control and ability to visualize a putt. You will develop the ability to mentally see-the-putt/feel-the-putt.	Visualization				
	Control				
	Confidence				
	Versatility				
	Swing Feel				
2 Alphabet Soup (On Green)	**Easy**				
You get points for putting accurately to different distances. • This helps you develop distance control and ability to visualize a putt.	Visualization				
	Control				
	Confidence				
	Versatility				
	Swing Feel				
3 Goal Post (On Green)	**Easy**				
A basic putting competition where you putt with your eyes closed through a goal made of two markers while attempting to hit a target. • This game helps you develop both distance and direction control. You'll learn to trust your putting stroke and make the transfer from practice green to golf course easier.	Visualization				
	Control				
	Confidence				
	Versatility				
	Swing Feel				

4 Croquet (On Green)	Easy			
A fun putting competition, similar to the game of croquet where you play through a series of four goals. • A great game to play with a group at various skill levels. Especially challenging to play as a speeded game.	Visualization			
	Control			
	Confidence			
	Versatility			
	Swing Feel			

5 Spiral (On Green)	Moderate			
Compete against another player to get a ball into a target from different directions and distances. • Spiral helps you develop speed and directional control as you putt from changing distances and directions to a single hole.	Visualization			
	Control			
	Confidence			
	Versatility			
	Swing Feel			

6 Hits the Spot (On Green)	Moderate			
Hit a ball through a single wicket to a target. • This game develops your ability to read greens for speed and pick the correct amount of break. This improves your visualization, putter face control, speed, and mechanics.	Visualization			
	Control			
	Confidence			
	Versatility			
	Swing Feel			

7 Jousting (On Green)	Difficult			
Compete against another player while simultaneously putting a ball to target holes. • A competition to help you learn how to putt under pressure.	Visualization			
	Control			
	Confidence			
	Versatility			
	Swing Feel			

8 Pin Up (On Green)	Moderate				
Compete by hitting balls from different spots located 3, 6, and 9 feet from a hole. • This puts you in game-like conditions to capture the pressure of having to make a putt. Also a great solitaire game to help you at the end of a practice session.	Visualization				
	Control				
	Confidence				
	Versatility				
	Swing Feel				

9 Putting Zigzag (On Green)	Moderate				
A fun game where you putt through a series of gates and sink the ball in a specific hole. • Helps you develop control over changing conditions on the green.	Visualization				
	Control				
	Confidence				
	Versatility				
	Swing Feel				

10 Last One Standing (On Green)	Moderate				
Players are eliminated for misses as they putt from increasing distances to a target hole. • Another game to enhance transfer to the course by providing competition while putting from various distances. Especially good for group competition.	Visualization				
	Control				
	Confidence				
	Versatility				
	Swing Feel				

11 GIMMIE (On Green)	Moderate				
A challenge competition where you get letters to the word Gimmie for putts made in one stroke. Try to play against another player of equal or better ability. • Helps you putt under competitive pressure, challenging your competitive spirit and improving your concentration. An especially good game to practice your pre-shot routine to establish a consistent swing under pressure.	Visualization				
	Control				
	Confidence				
	Versatility				
	Swing Feel				

12 Speed Putting (On Green)	Difficult			
A timed game where you putt four balls to a hole within a set time limit. • A fun game to help you to putt confidently under pressure. It creates trust in your basic putting stroke. It forces you to minimize the overthinking that prevents a good putter from becoming a great putter.	Visualization			
	Control			
	Confidence			
	Versatility			
	Swing Feel			
13 Match Putting (On Green)	**Difficult**			
A match play game where you compete against another player to win the most holes over a nine-hole course. • A competition to help you learn how to strategize and putt under pressure.	Visualization			
	Control			
	Confidence			
	Versatility			
	Swing Feel			

B. Putting FROM OFF the Green (4 Games)

These games focus on putting from locations off the green—fringe, rough, and fairway. They also encourage using all clubs helpful in moving the ball to the hole.

PUTTING OFF THE GREEN GAMES	EVALUATION			
14 Arcade (Off Green)	**Easy**			
Compete against players when putting through a gap in a row of tees. • Arcade focuses on subtle changes needed to putt accurately to different targets at the same distance. The focus is on directional control.	Visualization			
	Control			
	Confidence			
	Versatility			
	Swing Feel			

15 Blackjack (Off Green)	Moderate				
Putt from off the green using a variety of clubs. • Use many clubs for this game! It develops your versatility when putting from off the green. It builds your confidence that you have several club choices when putting. (Yes, you can putt with something other than your putter!)	Visualization				
	Control				
	Confidence				
	Versatility				
	Swing Feel				
16 Mishmash (Off Green)	**Moderate**				
Compete putting from off the green, using a variety of clubs from four different locations. • By encouraging use of all your clubs, this game sharpens your putting skill, club selection, shot creation, green reading, and swing mechanics. The arsenal of shots developed here will enhance your skill with every club in your bag.	Visualization				
	Control				
	Confidence				
	Versatility				
	Swing Feel				
17 Up and In (Off Green)	**Moderate**				
Compete to sink balls from off the green in one or two strokes using clubs selected in advance. • Puts you into situations you will face when you need to score well. Puts a premium on scoring using a putting stroke while helping you develop a feel for putting with different clubs.	Visualization				
	Control				
	Confidence				
	Versatility				
	Swing Feel				

Chipping: The Scoring Game

Tom came to Matt, complaining that his golf game was not improving. He loved golf and played almost daily, but nothing seemed to get him out of scoring in the mid-90s. He seemed to be clueless about where the problems were.

So, Matt observed him on the practice range. Tom hit full shots that had single-digit handicap written all over them.

He smacked his driver 250 yards and farther. He said this was typical. His performance with his other clubs kept pace with his drives.

After a few more shots, they moved to the short game area where Tom hit a few balls from 5 and 10 yards from the green. He missed the green with every shot! He hit low line drives and then hit behind the ball, throwing in a few lateral shots for good measure.

Once on the green, his putting was good.

When asked if this was usual, Tom said "Yes." He rarely practiced short shots, because he did not know how to hit them. Tom took two lessons focusing on chipping and pitching technique.

Following the lessons, Matt assigned Tom play to play the basic chipping games—Between the Rails and In the Pits. Within a month, Tom's scores dropped dramatically, and his handicap fell from a 20 to 13.

A **chip** is a stroke in which you do not take a full swing and where your goal is to advance the ball by having it roll more than it flies. Most of the time, a chip is played from close to the green to get the ball to roll across the green and into the cup.

Reading this section and playing the games in the Chipping booklet will help you to:

- Understand the difference between a chip and a pitch.
- Understand when a chip is an appropriate shot.
- Learn about the games in the Chipping booklet so you will:
    - Develop a feel for both distance and directional control for chips close to the green.
    - Cultivate a feel for short chips with a variety of clubs.
    - Build confidence in long chips, using all of the clubs in your bag.

Introduction: The Chip

The **chip** is a basic skill shot that every golfer should master.

- Usually the chip is used when the ball is close to the green and you want to get up and down (one chip and one putt).
- Another situation for a chip is when you are in trouble and must hit a low shot that will run a long distance. An example is when you must hit under an overhanging tree limb to advance the ball toward the green.

Games in this section include both shots.

Unless you are an incredibly good player, not all of your approach shots land on the green! If your ball lands in a sand bunker, you have a specialty shot to make (see Chapter 6).

> The [chip shot is] one stroke that marks the difference between fame and oblivion.
>
> — Samuel L. Parrish, USGA official

So you must make a decision: Should I hit a shot that lands the ball close to the hole and stops, or should I hit a shot that lands well in front of the hole and then rolls to it?

Traditional wisdom is to roll the ball whenever you can. This means think putt first, then chip, and finally pitch. One reason the chip is preferred to the pitch is that the more lofted shot tends to have more room for error, while the rolling chip has a higher probability of running into the hole. Yet this wisdom should be considered carefully.

We recommend that you chip when you have the following conditions:

- You are close to the green, there are no obstructions between you and the hole, you have a clean lie, and the path to the hole is relatively flat. A chip is most effective under these conditions.
- You are far from the green and there is some overhanging obstruction that blocks you from hitting a shot that rises into the air, so you have to make a low shot that rolls a good distance. An example would be hitting a ball under a tree branch.

- You are caught off the fairway, cannot make a full swing, and have no clear shot to the green. Here you need to get the ball back in play by hitting a low shot that rolls to a spot where you have a safer approach to the pin.

Do not chip under this condition:

- There is an obstruction between you and the hole, such as a bunker, tree, bush, pond, or creek. Instead of chipping, make a shot that gets airborne, lands on the green, and stops close to the hole. This is a pitch. The pitch will fly farther than it rolls. We cover pitching in the next section.

Tech Talk: Chipping

Rollout is the distance a ball rolls after it hits the ground. Since the goal of the chip on the green is to get the ball rolling quickly it is important to understand how far the ball will fly and how far it will roll.

The amount of rollout depends on your swing, the club's loft, loft delivered to the ball, and the slope, firmness, and speed of the green. Clearly, level chips will roll farther than uphill chips.

The following table gives the approximate distances a ball will roll on a level green based on club selection. Since there is some variation in the loft of similar clubs based on the manufacturer's design, you should spend time learning how far balls will roll based on ball position, your swing set-up, the balls you use, and your clubs.

Slope of the green	Club	Air-to-Roll Ratio		Distance for 24-Yard Chip	
		Air	Roll	Air	Roll
Level	6-iron	1:4	3:4	6	18
	8-iron	1:3	2:3	8	16
	Pitching wedge	1:2	1:2	12	12
Uphill	4-iron	1:4	1:4	6	18
	6-iron	1:3	2:3	8	16
	8-iron	1:2	1:2	12	12
Downhill	8-iron	1:4	3:4	6	18
	Pitching Wedge	1:3	2:3	8	16
	Lob Wedge	1:2	1:2	12	12

Rollout distances for a variety of clubs

Source: http://golf.about.com/od/golftips/ss/6_8_10_chipping.htm

When you evaluate how far the ball rolls with each club, be sure to use the same swing and ball position in your stance. Also, it's important to play with clubs that are fitted to your size and swing. This will give you the consistency that is vital to an effective short game.

Since different clubs give you a shot that varies in height, distance, and roll, uniformity in technique with the clubs will give you the consistency you need to succeed on the course. If you play our games, you will develop a repeatable shot.

To emphasize the impact that hitting close to the pin has on scores, Ken Tanner summarized the relationship between the distance from the pin and the typical score for average golfers. We summarize his results in the following figure.

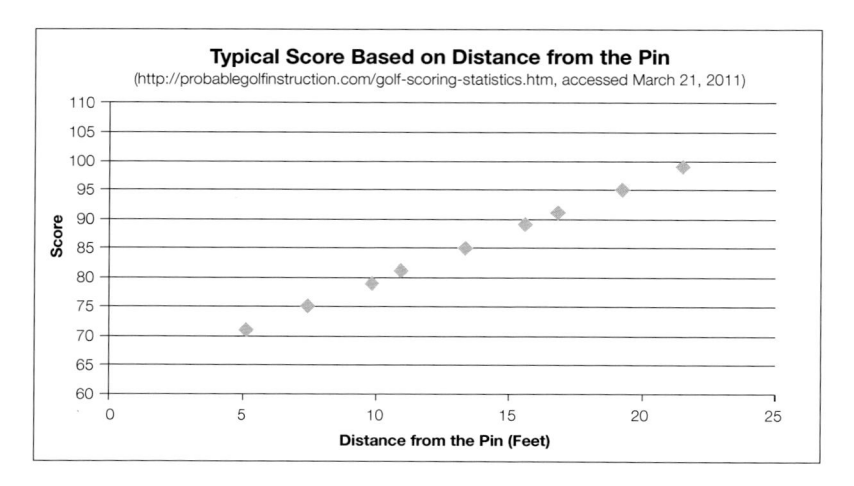

Typical Score Based on Distance from the Pin
(http://probablegolfinstruction.com/golf-scoring-statistics.htm, accessed March 21, 2011)

These results illustrate that getting the ball close to the pin has a direct impact on a player's total score. Players consistently hitting the ball 20 feet from the pin typically score in the mid-90s. Reducing this distance by only five feet typically results in scores in the mid-80s. This is quite a difference! The message here is that the closer your short game shots are to the pin, the lower your score can be.

Your Go-To Club

The well-executed chip can be a round-savior; the poorly executed one can be a round-killer. It is important that you gain confidence in one club that you can count on when chipping, and then practice with it often. One way you can do this is to take several irons (sand wedge, pitching wedge, 9-iron, and 8-iron) and spend time chipping with them. Take the one that you can hit most consistently and commit to this club as your go-to club for chipping.

Games that require you to make the same chip using different clubs include *Chipping: Up and Down* and *Chipping Trifecta*. Try them!

Short Chipping Games (1–15 yards)

You can think of the "short chip" as a "long putt" where the ball flies a short distance and then rolls to the cup. This is a key finesse shot you should master.

Our short chipping games give you experience using a variety of clubs to chip a short distance to the green. The first games help you acquire skill with distance, direction, and control. The rest are more advanced and focus on chipping and holing the ball in as few strokes as possible. These are the up-and-down shots. (**H**) indicates games you can play at home.

Note: If you play these games alone, it is important that you move to a variety of positions rather than chipping consistently from the same location.

A. Short Chipping (16 Games)

SHORT CHIPPING GAMES	EVALUATION				
1 Chipping in the Dark (Short Chip)	Easy				
Chip to a marker or hole with your eyes closed. • The primary goal is to *develop your distance control and ability to visualize and feel a chip.* This game improves your ability to mentally see and feel a chip.	Visualization				
	Control				
	Confidence				
	Versatility				
	Swing Feel				
2 Basket Ball (H) (Short Chip)	Easy				
Beginning chipping competition where you chip the ball into a basket. • The focus is on *basic chipping stroke.* It helps with learning alignment, swing speed, body position, club, ball, and target relationships.	Visualization				
	Control				
	Confidence				
	Versatility				
	Swing Feel				

3 Between-the-Rails (Short Chip)	Easy			
A slightly more advanced chipping competition, where you chip and have the ball run between two rails or guides. • The focus is *direction control*. It also helps with learning alignment, body position, club, ball, and target relationships.	Visualization			
	Control			
	Confidence			
	Versatility			
	Swing Feel			
4 Chipping Leapfrog (H) (Short Chip)	Easy			
Chipping competition where you get points for chipping and landing the ball in a target area. • The focus is on *fine-tuning distance control* when hitting to a target area. It also gives you a sense of rollout.	Visualization			
	Control			
	Confidence			
	Versatility			
	Swing Feel			
5 Beginning Line-'Em-Up (Short Chip)	Moderate			
Chipping competition where you chip over a guard club to three target tees. • The focus is *basic chipping mechanics, distance, and direction control*. It helps you learn alignment, body position, club, ball, and target relationships.	Visualization			
	Control			
	Confidence			
	Versatility			
	Swing Feel			
6 Line-'Em-Up: The Front Nine (Short Chip)	Moderate			
Slightly more advanced than Beginning Line-'Em-Up. Players chip to changing targets and distances using a variety of clubs. • Focuses on distance and directional control. You get a feel for how different clubs behave in similar situations, and identify those that work best for you in different playing situations.	Visualization			
	Control			
	Confidence			
	Versatility			
	Swing Feel			

7 In the Pits (Short Chip)	Moderate				
Chip over an obstacle to a target hole. • Helps you *get a feel for the distance a ball will roll out* after chipping to a target spot. It helps you develop a sense of distance control as you learn how the ball reacts with different lofted clubs. The pit is a hazard, and this game helps you overcome any mental demons when chipping over them.	Visualization				
:::	Control				
:::	Confidence				
:::	Versatility				
:::	Swing Feel				

8 Take Ten (Short Chip)	Moderate				
Compete to get the ball up and down as many times as you can within ten strokes. • Helps you focus on *accuracy.* You will gain confidence in your swing and learn how to compete under pressure.	Visualization				
:::	Control				
:::	Confidence				
:::	Versatility				
:::	Swing Feel				

9 Chipping: Up and Down (Short Chip)	Moderate				
Compete to get the ball up and down in one or two strokes when chipping from off the green. • This is the first of several score-lowering games. Use different clubs and learn how to vary your technique to get the ball up and down, a skill essential for low scoring. It also helps you identify your go-to club for chipping.	Visualization				
:::	Control				
:::	Confidence				
:::	Versatility				
:::	Swing Feel				

10 Chipping Rollout (Short Chip)	Moderate				
You get points for chipping to different distances. • Helps you *visualize rollout* and develop an automatic feel by chipping to targets at different distances.	Visualization				
:::	Control				
:::	Confidence				
:::	Versatility				
:::	Swing Feel				

11 Chipping Zigzag (Short Chip)	Moderate			
A combination game where you chip to the green, putt through a series of gates, and hole out in as few strokes as possible. • Similar to *Putting Zigzag*. You develop both *a feel for chipping to a target and putting to a variety of distances.* It is primarily a distance control game that combines target selection, distance control, and accuracy.	Visualization			
	Control			
	Confidence			
	Versatility			
	Swing Feel			

12 Speed Chipping (Short Chip)	Moderate			
Chip eight balls to a target within a time limit. • Gain confidence as you develop an *automatic chipping stroke*. It helps you chip without overanalyzing the shot.	Visualization			
	Control			
	Confidence			
	Versatility			
	Swing Feel			

13 Bump and Run (Short Chip)	Difficult			
Chip to a target area and have the ball run to a target. • An advanced game that develops your skill to *chip to a specific spot and have the ball run to a target.* Perfecting your ability here gives you one of the basic short game shots that will lower your score.	Visualization			
	Control			
	Confidence			
	Versatility			
	Swing Feel			

14 Chipping Trifecta (Short Chip)	Difficult			
Compete to sink balls from off the green in the fewest strokes using different clubs for each shot. • Promotes imagination and confidence with *several clubs*. It helps you become proficient with more than one club when chipping from the same lie, helps you work out of unusual situations, adds a new dimension to your short game, and helps you gain confidence in a go-to club.	Visualization			
	Control			
	Confidence			
	Versatility			
	Swing Feel			

15 Match Chipping (Short Chip)	Difficult				
Match play game where you compete against another player to win the most holes by chipping up and in. • Helps you *close out holes under pressure*. It simulates the competitive pressure you may feel in a competitive tournament.	Visualization				
	Control				
	Confidence				
	Versatility				
	Swing Feel				
16 Shorty (Short Chip)	Difficult				
Practice making short-sided chips out of the greenside rough to a hole on the green. • Emphasizes one of the most demanding touch shots, the *short chip out of the greenside rough*. Playing it develops your skill with this difficult shot.	Visualization				
	Control				
	Confidence				
	Versatility				
	Swing Feel				

B. Long Chips and Recovery Shots (5 Games)

These games build experience with hitting long chips and hitting out of trouble to a target in the fairway.

LONG CHIPPING GAMES	EVALUATION				
17 Shank (Long Chip)	Easy				
Play long chip shots to a target. • Helps you develop the *distance control* every player needs when hitting low, controlled shots. It strengthens swing pace, length, and clubface control. Helps you to decide the go-to club when confronted with similar shots on the course.	Visualization				
	Control				
	Confidence				
	Versatility				
	Swing Feel				

18 Olympic Shank (Long Chip)	Moderate			
Hit long chip shots to the same target using a variety of clubs. • Helps you develop *distance control* when using a variety of golf club lofts and swing speeds. Helps you develop skills you need to make recovery shots when you are in trouble.	Visualization			
	Control			
	Confidence			
	Versatility			
	Swing Feel			
19 Under the Weather (Long Chip)	**Moderate**			
Chip under an obstruction to a target using a variety of clubs. • Gives you *experience making long chips under obstacles to get out of trouble.* To gain full value, use both low and high lofted clubs as you hit the ball under a hurdle.	Visualization			
	Control			
	Confidence			
	Versatility			
	Swing Feel			
20 Troublesome (Long Chip)	**Difficult**			
Players chip from a restricted area to different targets, using a variety of clubs. • *Simulates trouble shots you might face on the course.* Gives you experience hitting controlled shots from confined lies. It can be played as an on-course game.	Visualization			
	Control			
	Confidence			
	Versatility			
	Swing Feel			
21 Thread the Needle (Long Chip)	**Difficult**			
Make long chips under and through a pair of stakes to different targets, using a variety of clubs. • *Simulates trouble shots you might face on the course when having to make long chips through trees.* Gives you experience with hitting controlled shots from confined lies. Can be played as an on-course game.	Visualization			
	Control			
	Confidence			
	Versatility			
	Swing Feel			

Pitching: Up and Away

Joel was a good junior player. He and Matt, his coach, were preparing for his first national tournament, where the rough would be severe and unforgiving. Matt showed Joel a muff shot designed to control a ball out of high grass, playing the games Swamp Monster and Three Ball. They would compete against each other for hours hitting out of the worst possible lies. After playing these games for several weeks, Joel had developed confidence both in the shot and how to execute it in the stress of a highly competitive tournament.

Pitch: a stroke where you do not take a full swing and the ball flies more than it rolls. The goal is to get the ball close to the hole.

Reading this section and playing the games in the Pitching booklet will help you to:

- Understand when to pitch the ball.
- Learn about the games in the Pitching booklet so you will:
    - Become more skilled in controlling the accuracy of your pitches.
    - Develop a feel for of how each of your lofted clubs will work for you.
    - Increase confidence in a go-to club for pitches.

Introduction: Pitch Shots

This chapter focuses on using lofted clubs close to the green. Most of us end up with shots to the green where a chip is not appropriate. There may be a bunker we need to hit over, a creek or pond in our path, a bush or tree in the way, or simply gnarly, uneven ground we would like to avoid.

In this situation we need to fly the ball a relatively short distance, between 5 and 50 yards, using a lofted club and an abbreviated swing. We want the ball to hit the green and stop quickly. This is a **pitch,** the second of the finesse shots that all golfers should master.

*(**Note:** Technically, almost any shot you take from the fairway to the green using an abbreviated swing could be thought of as being a pitch.)*

Pitches are among the trickiest shots to master since direction and distance control are essential for successful execution. Along with the chip, a pitch is the shot that can either save or sink a round. Unfortunately, most players do not practice pitches enough relying instead on the drive and the full-swing approach shot to get to the green. The nice thing about the short pitch is that it is a shot you can rehearse at home (as long as you don't mind chewing up the lawn a bit).

When Should I Pitch?

As we have said, for most close-in shots your priority should be to putt, then chip, then pitch. There are situations where you should choose a lofted shot. You should pitch when:

- There is some obstruction between your ball and the ideal landing spot on the green and you need to have the ball stop relatively quickly when it hits the green.
- You are fairly close to the green and the ball is in the deep rough.
- You are just off the green, the ball is in the deep rough, and you are close to the hole.
- You are 10 to 50 yards from the green and the green is not level, making a chip a more risky shot.

You should not pitch if you have the following condition:

- You have a short shot with an unobstructed approach to the green, and the ground between you and the pin is relatively level. In this case a chip or long putt is a better choice.

Tech Talk: Pitching

As we said in the chipping section, rollout is the distance a ball rolls after it hits the ground. For a well-executed pitch, the ball will fly more than it rolls.

The following table gives the approximate distance a ball will fly and roll when hit with each of the lofted clubs.

Keep in mind that the rollout depends on the loft of the club, the position of the ball in your stance, the type of ball you use, and your swing. Other issues to keep in mind are the amount of moisture in the green (balls stop faster on wet, soft greens) and the slope of the ground where the ball lands. Level pitches will roll a bit farther than uphill pitches.

The example in this table is for an *expert* golfer hitting to a moderately fast green. Since there is some variation in the loft of every club, based on the manufacturer's design, there will be some variation in these distances.

You should spend time learning how far you hit with each of your lofted clubs. The self-assessments in Chapter 9 will help you do this.

Typical rollout for pitches (*expert*)				
Club	**Total Yards Hit**	**Air-to-Roll Percent***	
		Air	Roll
60 Degree Lob Wedge	10	70%	30%
	30	80%	20%
	50	90%	10%
56 Degree Sand Wedge	10	65%	35%
	30	75%	25%
	50	90%	10%
52 Degree Gap Wedge	10	60%	40%
	30	70%	30%
	50	85%	15%
48 Degree Pitching Wedge	10	50%	50%
	30	65%	35%
	50	80%	20%
* The stronger the swing, the less roll you can expect.			

A. Short Pitches (5–20 yards) (14 Games)

The following 14 games help you gain confidence in short pitches. The capital **H** indicates games that can be played at home. If you play these games alone, move to a variety of positions rather than pitching consistently from the same location.

SHORT PITCHING GAMES	EVALUATION

1 High Ball (H) (Short Pitch)

Easy

An easy, short pitching competition where you pitch into a box or basket.

- Helps you with the basic pitching stroke. This game will reinforce correct alignment, swing speed, body position, and club, ball, and target relationships.

Visualization				
Control				
Confidence				
Versatility				
Swing Feel				

2 Levitation (H) (Short Pitch)

Easy

An easy, short pitching competition where you compete to hit a ball over an obstacle.

- Helps you visualize a ball's flight when you use lofted clubs. Also helps you develop swing pace, swing length, and clubface control. Also lets you determine your go-to club for the variety of short distances you will encounter on the course.

Visualization				
Control				
Confidence				
Versatility				
Swing Feel				

3 Over and Under (H) (Short Pitch)

Moderate

An advanced form of Levitation, where you compete to hit a ball over and then under a hurdle, using the same club.

- Helps you learn to control ball flight by changing your swing, ball position, and loft of the club. Also lets you understand that the same club can be used for hitting both high and low shots.

Visualization				
Control				
Confidence				
Versatility				
Swing Feel				

4 Pitching Leapfrog (H) (Short Pitch)

Easy

A beginning pitching competition where you get points for pitching over an obstruction and land the ball in a target area.

- Helps you gain confidence when pitching over an obstacle with the goal of hitting a landing point. Develops a sense of accuracy and control for lofted shots.

Visualization				
Control				
Confidence				
Versatility				
Swing Feel				

5 Pitching Rollout (Short Pitch)	Easy				
You get points for pitching to different distances. • Develops your understanding of and feel for rollout, and helps you develop distance and direction control.	Visualization				
	Control				
	Confidence				
	Versatility				
	Swing Feel				
6 Target Practice (H) (Short Pitch)	Easy				
Another easy, short pitching competition where you pitch to a target using a lofted club. • Learn to control the distance the ball travels by using different swing speeds and clubs with different lofts. Learn how to vary the length of your swing to create long and short pitches.	Visualization				
	Control				
	Confidence				
	Versatility				
	Swing Feel				
7 Swamp Monster (H) (Short Pitch)	Moderate				
Compete by pitching over a "swamp" to a target. • Helps you with distance and directional control when hitting over obstacles. Develops both touch and feel from different locations and understanding of how both the speed of the club and the loft of the face can complement each other to influence ball flight and rollout.	Visualization				
	Control				
	Confidence				
	Versatility				
	Swing Feel				
8 Safe and Sorry (Short Pitch)	Moderate				
A variation of Swamp Monster, where you pitch eight balls to a target within a set time limit. • Helps you develop shots needed to loft the ball and stop it close to a target on the green. Learn how to vary the loft of different clubs to get ball up in the air and land softly. The game's time pressure helps you gain confidence in your stroke without overthinking.	Visualization				
	Control				
	Confidence				
	Versatility				
	Swing Feel				

9 Pitch Off the Old Block (Short Pitch) — Moderate

Pitch over an obstacle to get ball close to hole using a variety of clubs.

- Another game to help you develop lofted shots over obstacles and hazards and get ball to stop close to a target on the green.

Visualization				
Control				
Confidence				
Versatility				
Swing Feel				

10 Up and In (Short Pitch) — Moderate

Compete to get ball up and down in one or two strokes when pitching from off the green.

- Up-and-In combines pitching accuracy with putting skill. By putting a premium on scoring, you learn how to relax in similar situations on the course. This game is particularly helpful for golfers who normally play in competitive situations.

Visualization				
Control				
Confidence				
Versatility				
Swing Feel				

11 Three Ball (Short Pitch) — Difficult

Compete to pitch and putt out from off the green in the fewest strokes from three locations.

- Develop skill with a variety of lofted clubs, because you have to hit to the green from the same location using different clubs. *Three Ball* emphasizes the up-and-down shots you would normally find on the course.

Visualization				
Control				
Confidence				
Versatility				
Swing Feel				

12 Uneven Ground (Short Pitch) — Difficult

Pitch balls to targets from a variety of uphill, downhill, and side hill lies from the fairway and the rough.

- Introduces the uneven lies you will encounter on the course. Practicing hard shots expands your comfort zone with a variety of clubs and lies. Play harder shots than you think you will encounter on the course.

Visualization				
Control				
Confidence				
Versatility				
Swing Feel				

13 Pitching Zigzag (Short Pitch)	Moderate				
A fun game where you pitch to the green, putt through a series of gates, and sink the ball in a specific hole. • A game to help you to pitch to a target and develop control over changing conditions on the green.	Visualization				
	Control				
	Confidence				
	Versatility				
	Swing Feel				
14 Match Pitching (Short Pitch)	Moderate				
A match play game where you compete against another player to win the most holes over a nine-hole course. • The competition helps you pitch and putt up and down under pressure.	Visualization				
	Control				
	Confidence				
	Versatility				
	Swing Feel				

B. Long Pitching (15–50 yards) (5 Games)

A long pitch is really a short approach shot which requires you to master hitting the ball with less than a full swing. These games allow you to get a feel for these shots. They help you develop a preference for your go-to club for the 15–50 yard shot to the green.

LONG PITCHING GAMES	EVALUATION				
15 Air Mail (H) (Long Pitch)	Easy				
Compete in getting the ball close to a target 15–50 yards away. • Teaches how to hit to targets using less than a full swing. Develop clubface control, swing speed, and body control. By using many clubs, you figure out your go-to club for intermediate-distance pitch shots.	Visualization				
	Control				
	Confidence				
	Versatility				
	Swing Feel				

16 On-the-Edge (Long Pitch)	Moderate				
Practice making short-sided pitches from an intermediate distance. • The major focus is distance control. *On-the-Edge* helps you develop skill in making shots that need to fly the ball a controlled distance to a green and then stop quickly.	Visualization				
	Control				
	Confidence				
	Versatility				
	Swing Feel				
17 Skyze (H) (Long Pitch)	**Moderate**				
An advanced pitching competition where you hit the ball to different targets using a different club for each shot from 15–50 yards away. • Helps you develop an automatic swing when hitting to intermediate distances with different clubs.	Visualization				
	Control				
	Confidence				
	Versatility				
	Swing Feel				
18 Fall Back (Long Pitch)	**Moderate**				
Make short and long pitches hitting to a target while systematically increasing the distance to it. • Highly competitive game that develops feel, touch, and distance control. Performance through competition is a great way to develop an automatic shot and gain confidence in your swing.	Visualization				
	Control				
	Confidence				
	Versatility				
	Swing Feel				
19 Long Shot (Long Pitch)	**Moderate**				
Compete getting up and down from distances greater than 15 yards. • Develops your ability to plan and visualize a shot. Takes you out of your comfort zone, since you will use different lofted clubs and create a variety of shots to score in a competitive setting.	Visualization				
	Control				
	Confidence				
	Versatility				
	Swing Feel				

5
Full Swing: Tee and Approach Shots

Reading This chapter will help you to:

- Understand that length is not absolutely necessary to lowering your golfing score.
- Become aware of the keys to an effective tee shot.
- Understand the variation in club design and how this affects distance.

When practicing, most golfers focus on full swing shots, and most golfing lessons are devoted to mastering it. This chapter is devoted to games that will help you develop a feel for hitting these shots consistently and confidently.

Full Swing: Off the Tee

Matt was teaching Jim, an aspiring tour professional in Florida, who was having trouble hitting the fairway with his driver. Jim's lack of confidence was so strong that he was ready to give up golf as a career.

On the practice tee, each iron shot was a bullet: solid, crisp. They flew beautifully. But when he shifted to the driver, he couldn't hit the practice range. Matt took him to a spot overlooking the beach and told him to "hit the ocean." Jim looked at Matt quizzically. Matt repeated, "Just hit it into the water."

When Jim asked where in the ocean, Matt replied, "Just hit it in the ocean!" Jim proceeded to hit prodigious drives, one after another, without any hesitation. He asked why this was working.

Matt replied, "You are letting your real swing work for you, just like you let your real swing work with your approach shots. Picture every tee shot like you are hitting into the ocean, and don't let the results worry you."

To reinforce this free feeling, Matt told Jim to play Speedy Tee (Full Swing booklet) four times every time he practiced. Jim proceeded to shoot 68 in the next round, and wound up finishing ninth in his next tournament.

> **Tee shot:** any shot made from the tee box. The goal is to either advance the ball down the fairway or, for par-three holes, to hit the green.

Reading this section and playing the games in the Full Swing booklet will help you to:

- Increase your awareness of the need for planning and course management for tee shots.
- Learn about the games in the *Full Swing Booklet* so you will:
    - Improve your feel for directional control for tee shots.
    - Gain a sense of distance control off the tee.
    - Find your optimal tee height when hitting from the tee box.
    - Instill confidence in a full, free swing when hitting a driver.

Introduction: The Tee Shot

It is essential to master the tee shot to maximize your ability to play golf well. You will tee off eighteen times during a round—that is the only sure thing in golf. Since this is an inevitable shot, here are some suggestions for effective shots off the tee.

The key to effective tee shots is to ***play within yourself.*** Know what you can do, and play your game. Don't try to match the shots of a power hitter. If you are playing with someone who feels that it is their duty to shatter the ball with every drive, let them play their game.

Being content with your shots will help you **enjoy *your* game**. A basic truth: *people drive for show; chipping, pitching, and putting put you in the dough.*

Always consider three key things when teeing off:

1. **Be accurate.** Everyone thinks that length is the goal of every tee shot. This may be true for longer holes, but it may not be desirable for par-three holes or shorter par-four holes where you need to lay up to an ideal distance for your second shot. In these cases, *accuracy* is vital, not length.

2. **Have directional control.** Distance without accuracy gets you into deep trouble. Many of us have struggled with a slice or hook that would make a boomerang blush. Hitting on-line is as important as hitting long.

3. **Know your target.** Knowing where you will hit the ball distinguishes the excellent golfer from the adequate one. Every drive needs a target area. Choose your target where you know your next shot will either get you to the green while avoiding hazards, or will put you in a place where the next shot will be in your comfort zone. Shot selection from the tee is as important as it is from a deep lie in the rough 20 yards from the green.

> Getting a hole-in-one is pretty rare. For a pro, the odds are 1 in 3,756; for the typical Sunday player, the odds are 1 in 12,750.

All three of these are important to a good driving game. If you are a *beginner* or *occasional* player, you may struggle with consistent distance and directional control. But keep your focus on the shot that, for you, will maximize the chance that your next will be a winner.

Tech Talk: Off the Tee

There are key decisions you must make when hitting off the tee: *A. Which club should I use? B. How high should I place the tee? C. What ball should I use?*

A. Which Club Should I use?

Which club to use depends on how well you play, the distance and accuracy with which you hit the ball, and the length and shape of the fairway leading to the hole. Club manufacturers make endless claims about their drivers and their ability to hit a ball long and straight. There are more claims for the benefits of driving clubs than there are bubbles in champagne.

For *skilled* players, there may be legitimate reasons for selecting one club over another. But this is not true for everyone. For average players, here are key considerations when choosing a driver:

- **Have your driver professionally fitted to match your swing pattern.** Also, the shaft flexibility should match your swing speed. Discuss this with your coach, or teacher, or a professional clubfitter. These people are best qualified to match your club to your swing.
- **Match the loft of your driver to your strength and ability to hit the ball.** The higher the loft, the more forgiving the club. Strong, *skilled* players can hit drivers with lofts less than 10 degrees. Players with less swing speed should use drivers with higher lofts.
- **Do not feel compelled to hit with a driver off the tee.** In fact, many players hit other clubs. Feel free to tee off with a 15 degree club, an 18 degree fairway metal, or a 25 degree hybrid. For *beginners,* we recommend that you start driving training with a 3-metal, 5-wood, or a driver built for your swing potential. With their higher lofts and shorter shafts, these clubs are much better suited for a player who is developing a swing.

> It is good sportsmanship not to pick up a ball while it is still rolling.
>
> —Mark Twain

Remember, the type of club you use does not matter as long as you are successful with it.

B. How High Should I Place the Tee?

An often overlooked decision is selecting the optimal tee height and placement in your stance. Here are suggestions:

- **Consistent tee height** is essential to a repeatable tee shot. For *beginning* and *occasional* players, using pre-marked tees, or marking the tees with a pen, is a good way to ensure consistency.
- **Tee the ball** higher and farther forward in your stance to maximize distance. Tee the ball lower for more control.
- **As you tee the ball higher,** move the position farther forward in your stance.
- **The size and loft of your club** will help you to determine how high to tee your ball. With a driver, tee the ball high and as far forward as you feel comfortable. In this case, use your lead foot as a guide. Tee the ball lower when hitting an iron, hybrid, or fairway metal.
- **To tee or not to tee?** On shorter par-3 holes, some better players prefer to play the ball from the ground when they hit an iron, hybrid, or fairway metal from the tee. Other players will follow the advice of the greatest player of all, Jack Nicklaus, who advises to tee the ball whenever it is permitted.
- **Tee the ball whenever or wherever you want,** both in the tee box and on the fairway. This is one way to have fun as a *beginning* golfer. Later you can "graduate" to limiting tee usage to starting each hole as you gain more confidence with your swing.
- **Include placing the tee** in your pre-shot routine.

C. What Ball Should I Use?

There is a bewildering variety of golf balls with impressive names and claims of improving your golf game. Thankfully, golfers no longer have to deal with leather balls stuffed with goose feathers, or ones made from gutta percha (a hard latex used in the 1800s), or liquid center balata-covered balls you discarded if hit with an iron in the middle (the club cut through the cover, giving the ball a distinctive smile). But enough ancient history! Golf balls today are more robust.

Your ball choice is about lowering your score, not about distance.

The best place to determine the right ball for your game is on the course, where you can try all your shots. Scoring shots—those made around the green using pitches, chips and putts—are just as important as hitting mile-long drives. All modern balls can deliver distance, but you will shoot lower scores with a ball that provides optimal overall *spin*—the spin that gives you best results with short irons and wedges. These are the scoring shots.

There are three basic elements to the modern golf ball: its core, its cover, and its dimple design. Manufacturers are constantly tinkering with these to develop balls with different characteristics that affect distance, spin, and feel when hit. Here are some hints for choosing a ball to fit your game.

- **Beginners.** *It really doesn't matter what kind of ball you select as a beginner.* However, stay away from old balls lying around someone's closet—these are quite unforgiving. Also, avoid balls used at most driving ranges, which are made of cement and have a different feel than balls used on the course. Buy balls you are not afraid to lose.

- **Occasional** and **Skilled** **players.** *Choose balls that best fit your game's needs.* If you play infrequently, then the decision is economic. Why spend $48.00 for a dozen balls that you won't use or won't improve your game? Ask your coach or golf professional which ball will best match your game. As your game progresses, choose the ball that best fits your swing speed and short game ability, and play with it consistently.

- **Expert players.** *Highly skilled golfers spend more time matching the ball to their game.* If you are a strong hitter, find a ball that is comfortable on all occasions. If you are a less-powerful hitter, choose a ball that maximizes carry and feel. Compare a few balls while playing. Consider the ball's feel off the driver, rescue clubs, irons. Experiment with short shots and putts and determine which ball helps your game on the course. Determine which ball is best for you during live action play—not at the range or from a launch monitor. You may need to change balls according to the conditions of play—is it windy, wet, dry, hot, or cold? Choose the ball that matches the day's conditions.

Full Swing: Off the Tee (7 Games)

These games help develop your driving skill, regardless of your level. The easier ones are for *beginners* and *occasional* players who need to develop confidence and find an automatic swing. For the novice player who is just learning to drive the ball, we suggest you start playing these games using lofted clubs or even irons to get used to hitting from a tee.

Note: When you play these games alone, alternate through all the clubs you typically hit from the tee.

OFF THE TEE GAMES	EVALUATION				
1 Bee Line (Off the Tee)	Easy				
Drive to progressively more distant targets—working up to a full swing. • Helps you develop your swing and directional control when hitting off a tee. It puts a premium on technique, not power, and helps you gain confidence in this essential shot.	Visualization				
	Control				
	Confidence				
	Versatility				
	Swing Feel				
2 Hit the Fairway (Off the Tee)	Easy				
Hit to an imaginary fairway in the range. • Helps you to gain more confidence and enhance your feel for the swing when teeing off. Its focus on accuracy helps you gain a better feel for an accurate drive.	Visualization				
	Control				
	Confidence				
	Versatility				
	Swing Feel				
3 Teed Off (Off the Tee)	Easy				
Drive balls to a target using different clubs and tees set at different heights. • Experiment with different tee heights to determine your most comfortable height. This boosts your confidence and helps you become more consistent with tee shots.	Visualization				
	Control				
	Confidence				
	Versatility				
	Swing Feel				

4 Speedy Tee (Off the Tee)	Intermediate			
Hit 5 balls off a tee to a target area within a time limit. • This enhances your ability to hit freely and automatically. It helps you develop confidence to swing without overthinking the shot.	Visualization			
	Control			
	Confidence			
	Versatility			
	Swing Feel			
5 Variety Pack (Off the Tee)	**Moderate**			
Drive to a target hitting from a tee, using a variety of clubs. • This gets you comfortable hitting clubs to different distances. It develops confidence in club choice and shot selection.	Visualization			
	Control			
	Confidence			
	Versatility			
	Swing Feel			
6 Crooked (Off the Tee)	**Advanced**			
You are challenged to shape shots over a point and land balls in a target area. • This advanced game helps you develop confidence in shaping tee shots. Becoming confident in which shot is easiest for you enhances your ability to transfer it to the course. It is fun to see how far you can bend a ball and still be accurate.	Visualization			
	Control			
	Confidence			
	Versatility			
	Swing Feel			
7 Rip It (Off the Tee)	**Moderate**			
You are challenged to drive balls off a tee. Each shot must be progressively farther than the previous one. • This game encourages you to let go of thoughts that interfere with performing well. It helps you increase your swing speed while helping you maintain control and put trust in your swing mechanics.	Visualization			
	Control			
	Confidence			
	Versatility			
	Swing Feel			

Full Swing: Approach Shots

Valerie Hogan, the wife of Ben Hogan, was listening to Ben one night after a round of golf. Ben was complaining that he could not make the putts necessary to play better golf. Without hesitation Valerie proceeded to tell Ben, "hit the ball closer!"

Approach shot: a shot from the fairway where the player takes a full swing with the goal of landing the ball on a specific target, usually the green.

Reading this section and playing the games in the *Full Swing Booklet* will help you to:

- Understand the relationship between your clubs and the distance you hit them.
- Learn about the fairway games in the *Full Swing Booklet* so you will:
  - Develop a feel for how you can hit each of your irons when making an approach shot.
  - Build a sense for what it feels like to hit a ball when hitting with less than a full swing using a full, three quarter, and half swing.
  - Become more confident when making long shots using all of the clubs in your bag.

Introduction: Getting to the Green

On longer holes, after their tee shot, golfers find themselves with a variety of options for either approaching or getting to the green. There are a number of ways to do this with either club or shot selection. A player with 150 yards to the green might try a moderately struck 6-iron, a hefty 7-iron, or even a lightly struck 5-iron. Any of these could be the correct choice depending on the weather, course, lie, and player's ability.

Players hitting from the fairway typically have one of two choices:

- **Hit the ball onto the green.** In this case there is a clear target. The decision here is to select the club that will fly the ball to the green and have it stop close to the pin. It is important to know which club will get you there comfortably *and* to have confidence in your shot selection. In golf, confidence breeds success.

- **Lay up to a place where the next shot has the best chance to get close to the pin.** The layup is a strategic decision. There are two times when this is a good choice:

  a. *You want to avoid a risky situation.* An example would be attempting a 190 yard shot over an obstacle when your chances of pulling it off are minimal. The better decision is to hit a shot short of the obstacle so that you have a shot you are confident you can make. Hitting to the safe yardage enables you to become aggressive with the next shot. This strategic fairway thinking will shave points off of your game.

  b. *You have a long shot to the green on a par-five hole.* You could decide to hit a 110 yard three wood to within 40 yards of the green and then hit a difficult touch shot to the pin. An alternative would be to hit the ball to a place where you can hit an easier full swing shot to the green. If the you have full confidence in the full swing shot, then the second option is the better choice. This is laying up to the go-to shot. Remember, play to your strong shot, not your hope-to-make shot.

Length Does Not Always Matter

Since fairway shots use a variety of clubs, it is important to know how far you can hit each one. This is essential to understanding your game. The smart player knows that **distance and direction must be blended**. It makes no sense to bash a 7-iron 175 yards and not know where it will land, when you can take a smoother swing and consistently hit this club 160 yards and feel confident that it will not be captured by either the rough or goblins living in the woods.

Key Point: It is not how far you can hit the ball; it is how close to your target you can hit it. Players who need to burn off energy or impress their teammates should do this in long ball competitions.

Tech Talk: Approach Shots

As we have said, the distance a ball flies is controlled by your swing, the shaft, the club's loft, and the type of ball. The higher the loft, the higher the ball will go and the shorter distance it will carry.

Many golfers assume that the loft of a 5-iron is the same for all manufacturers, and is the same today as it was for the same club thirty years ago. Nope! Many manufacturers, trying to impress golfers with their newest club design, have tweaked the loft almost as much as they have burnished the hosel. Lowering the loft of an 8-iron two degrees will increase the distance about six yards. Given an identical shaft, a change in 3 degrees of loft will add approximately nine yards in distance.

The next summarizes the differences in club lofts for four manufacturers. You can see that there is considerable variation in lofts among them. What does this mean for the average player? It is important to pick the clubs, shafts, and lofts that fit your swing. **Do not try to modify your swing to fit the club!**

Players with less flexibility might want to select a set that has higher, more forgiving features, such as perimeter weighting, lighter grips, and more flexible shafts. Stronger, more experienced players may choose cubs with lower lofts and stiffer shafts for more control and distance. This emphasizes the importance of having clubs fit to your swing and playing style.

Differences in Loft for Common Manufacturers*				
Club	Cobra SZ	Adams Idea A7	Titleist Z Blend	Cleveland Launcher
3-iron	20	19 (Hybrid)	21	20.5
4-iron	23	22 (Hybrid)	24	23
5-iron	26	25	27	26
6-iron	29	29	31	29
7-iron	32.5	33	35	33
8-iron	36	37	39	37
9-iron	40	41	43	41
Pitching wedge	44	45	47	45
*From manufacturers' data published in 2010.				

Reality Check: How Long Should I Be?

In our poll of golfing professionals, the one major mistake they comment on for *occasional* players is that they frequently under-club. They either overestimate how far the ball will fly, or they expect to hit the perfect shot rather than their typical shot. The better player has an accurate idea of how far he/she can hit each club under normal conditions. This should not be a wishful fantasy; it should be based on experience.

This table summarizes typical distances that average men and women can hit a ball using different clubs. These distances will vary based on your skill level, age, physical condition, experience, playing time, and course conditions. The three distances shown for amateurs (example: 200-230-260) represent typical yardages for short, intermediate, and long hitters.

How far can you hit the ball? After you have written in your distances, we can continue with your reality check.

For your reality check, we give you a structured way to determine your actual distances for your approach clubs in the *Full Swing Inventory* in Chapter 9. We recommend this self-assessment for players at all levels. It lets you know how accurate your distance expectations are. We also suggest that you do this assessment periodically, since our swings change as we get older, become more experienced, and learn more about our game of golf.

Typical Distances for Amateurs and Professional Players						
Club	Men*	Women*	LPGA**	PGA Players**	You?
Driver	200-230-260	150-175-200	246	294	
3-wood	180-215-235	125-150-180	218	260	
5-wood	170-195-210	105-135-170	200	242	
3-iron	160-180-200	100-125-160		220	
4--iron	150-170-185	90-120-150	180	209	
5-iron	140-160-170	80-110-140	170	198	

6-iron	130-150-160	70-100-130	159	185	
7-iron	120-140-150	65-90-120	147	177	
8-iron	110-130-140	60-80-110	135	162	
9-iron	95-115-130	55-70-95	123	149	
Pitching Wedge	80-105-120	50-60-80	109	137	
Sand Wedge	60-80-100	40-50-60			

*http://golf.about.com/od/beginners/l/blclubdistance.htm
**http://www.mytrackman.com/TrackMan.Online.DrivingRange/PGANumbers.html

One important note: your personal analysis should be done under your typical playing conditions. Weather and course conditions can have a dramatic effect on the distance your shot will carry. If it has been extremely dry, the course will be dry and shots onto the fairway and greens will roll farther. Cold and rain will reduce the length of a shot, and you may have to adjust by picking a longer club. And of course, wind will influence ball flight. Always be aware of wind direction when planning your shot.

A second element of your reality check is how accurate you expect to be when hitting to the green. The next graph summarizes how close to the pin all 192 PGA tour players were when hitting from the fairway at various distances. In 2010 the average distance from the pin when hitting from 50–75 yards was 15 feet. This would be a circle a little smaller than the average kitchen. These professional players hitting from 150–175 yards averaged 27.6 feet from the pin.

So, what does this mean for you?

- Expecting to stick the ball 4 feet from the flag with every approach shot is pretty unrealistic. Hoping to hit the green is more sensible.
- You should develop confidence in an approach club you can hit consistently with a full swing. You should be able to make this shot with poise, even if you are awakened from a sound sleep at 3 a.m. and asked to make it. This will be your go-to approach shot. When planning your course strategy, plan to lay up to this distance when hitting to the green.

FULL SWING: TEE AND APPROACH SHOTS

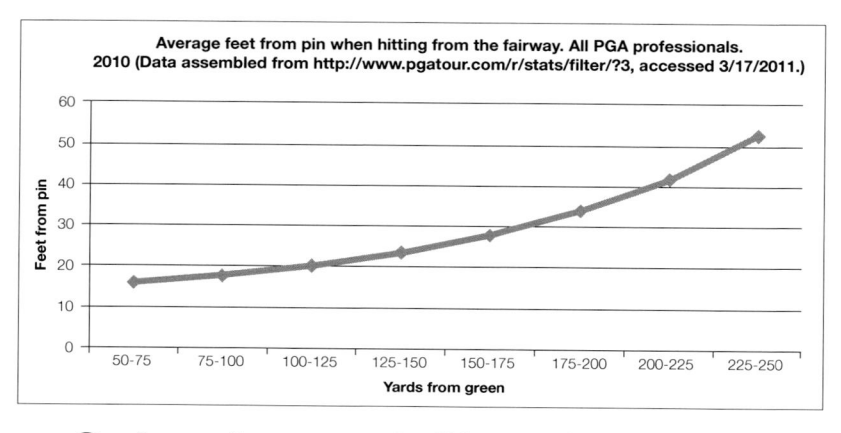

Average feet from pin when hitting from the fairway. All PGA professionals. 2010 (Data assembled from http://www.pgatour.com/r/stats/filter/?3, accessed 3/17/2011.)

Swing: Approach Shots (10 Games)

Our approach shot games begin with ones that focus on accuracy and distance control. Most can be played alone, and many can be played on the course.

APPROACH SHOT GAMES	EVALUATION				
8 Line Up (Approach)	**Easy**				
A beginning game where you take turns hitting a ball to a target line. • This helps you develop a feel for how accurately you can hit your clubs. Once you start to "stretch it out," you will develop confidence and skill hitting a full iron. You will also identify the point where you are swinging beyond your ability to control the shot.	Visualization				
	Control				
	Confidence				
	Versatility				
	Swing Feel				
9 Near and Far (Approach)	**Easy**				
Hit four balls along a target line. Each must be hit farther than the previous one without going beyond the target. • This is a distance control game that develops your skill and confidence in hitting accurately to various distances using less than a full swing.	Visualization				
	Control				
	Confidence				
	Versatility				
	Swing Feel				

10 Bull's-Eye (Approach)	Easy				
A beginning game that focuses on accuracy by requiring you to hit balls to a target area. • This game emphasizes accuracy and control. It helps you determine the distance you hit each club. As an easy competition, it matches the low level of pressure you might normally face in a friendly game.	Visualization				
	Control				
	Confidence				
	Versatility				
	Swing Feel				
11 Windmill (Approach)	Moderate				
Hit four balls to a target area as quickly as possible. • This helps you develop an automatic feel for hitting your approach shots. The time limit keeps you from overthinking each shot and reduces the mechanical thoughts that make taking your swing to the course difficult.	Visualization				
	Control				
	Confidence				
	Versatility				
	Swing Feel				
12 Liar (Approach)	Moderate				
Hit balls to a target from a variety of uphill, downhill, and sidehill lies. • This helps you develop proper posture and swing mechanics when making shots from uneven lies. It focuses on swing, posture, and balance adjustment. Playing it helps you become more feel-oriented and less mechanical when making these shots.	Visualization				
	Control				
	Confidence				
	Versatility				
	Swing Feel				
13 Roughing It (Approach)	Moderate				
Hit iron shots to targets from the rough. • Tour players hit 30% of their shots from the rough; you probably hit this area more often. This game helps you develop a feel for how the ball reacts when you hit it from different lies with different clubs.	Visualization				
	Control				
	Confidence				
	Versatility				
	Swing Feel				

14 Hacker (Approach)	**Moderate**				
Similar to the basketball game, Horse. You get letters to the word "Hacker" while competing to hit ball close to a target. • This game hones your shot skills in a friendly competition. It develops your ability to concentrate, focus, and manage emotional control.	Visualization				
	Control				
	Confidence				
	Versatility				
	Swing Feel				

15 Big Three (Approach)	**Moderate**				
Use a variety of clubs to hit to the same target using full and abbreviated swings. • A fun and demanding game, great for developing club control. Playing it enhances your sense of swing speed, loft, flight path, and visualization.	Visualization				
	Control				
	Confidence				
	Versatility				
	Swing Feel				

16 Grab Bag (Approach)	**Difficult**				
You are challenged to use different clubs to hit to the same target. • This helps you develop a feel for the variety of shots you can make with each iron. It helps you develop confidence and versatility while developing your comfort level with the distance you can hit each club.	Visualization				
	Control				
	Confidence				
	Versatility				
	Swing Feel				

17 Dictator (Approach)	**Difficult**				
Must be played with a partner. As you stand in your address position, your partner tells you how far to hit the ball mid-swing. • An excellent game for developing your concentration, balance, and club control.	Visualization				
	Control				
	Confidence				
	Versatility				
	Swing Feel				

6
Bunker Time

Rayann complained to Matt that she could not hit a bunker shot out of firm, wet sand. Her ball either rocketed across the green or she would "dig a ditch," leaving the ball in the bunker.

As fate would have it, just as they got to the practice bunker, it started to rain. The sand got firmer and firmer as the slight rain turned into a deluge. Rayann was determined to master the shot and proceeded to hit balls until she was comfortable with the swing technique she was working on.

The lesson took an hour. There was not enough Gore-Tex present to prevent them from becoming totally soaked, but to this day, Rayann is the master of firm sand.

Bunker shot: shot made from a hazard that is filled with sand.

Reading this chapter and playing the games in the *Bunker Booklet* will help you to:

- Understand why sand wedges are designed the way they are.
- Learn about the games in the *Bunker Booklet* so you will:
    - Hone your skill for getting out of greenside bunkers.
    - Develop a feel for how far the ball will fly and how far it will run with a sand wedge and other lofted clubs out of a greenside bunker.
    - Understand the difference between hitting out of soft sand and wet sand.
    - Improve your ability to hit out of fairway bunkers.

Introduction: Mastering the Bunker Shot

Other than hitting a 170 -yard shot across a gully full of nettles and wolverines to a green the size of a bath towel, there is no shot more nerve-wracking for the *beginning* and *occasional* player than one made out of sand.

The bunker shot is the only one where you do not have to hit the ball first to be successful. In addition, you cannot ground the club. While for many players this appears to be a tough, unpredictable shot, it is one that can be mastered with practice. The real difficulty is that the *greenside* bunker shot is *played differently* than the *fairway* bunker shot. Both require special instruction and practice.

Tech Talk: Bunker Shots

Golfing great Gene Sarazen developed the modern sand wedge in the early 1930s after seeing how an aircraft's tail adjusted while he was taking a flying lesson. The key characteristic of this wedge is its bounce or bounce angle. This refers to the angle between the sole of the club and the ground when the club is held vertically.

All clubs have some degree of bounce, depending on the club's loft, shape, and width of its sole. In the following figure the club on the left has a high degree of bounce— this is the extended sole at the back of the club that prevents it from digging into the sand. The club on the right has less bounce—it has a greater chance of digging into sand, preventing a clean shot.

Understanding bounce is pretty complex (a thorough discussion of bounce angle is in Jeff Summitt's Hireko Golf Blog, http://blog.hirekogolf.com/2007/10/understanding-golf-club-bounce-angle/).

What most golfers need to know is that the bounce angle of any club changes depending on two key factors:

- The angle is reduced the farther back in your stance you play the ball.
- When you open the club's face, the bounce angle increases. Closing the club face decreases the bounce. This is the reason that

golfers open the face when hitting out of soft sand. The increased bounce prevents the club from digging into the sand. Another way to look at this: the more you increase the loft of the club, the more you expose the bounce. Decreasing the loft minimizes the bounce.

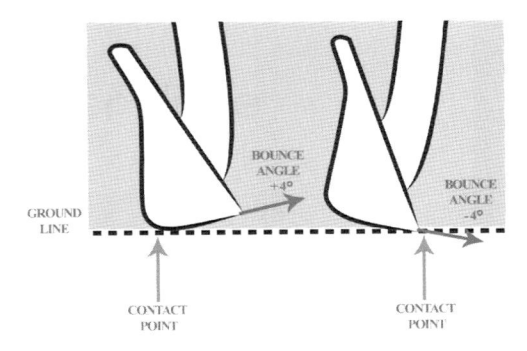

What Kind of Club Should I Use?

When you purchase a sand wedge, consider the amount of bounce. Your choice depends on the type of sand and turf you play. In soft sand, you will have greater success with more bounce on your club. But when bunkers are firm, less bounce is needed, since there is less opportunity for the club to dig in.

A. Greenside Bunker Games (12 Games)

Our first group of games focuses on the bunker shots you are most likely to face—those from a greenside bunker. If you are just beginning to learn these shots, we suggest that you get instruction on the basics before stepping into the sand. While making these shots is easier than you think, there are a couple of key adjustments you should make in your stance and swing to will make this shot easier to master.

GREENSIDE BUNKER GAMES	EVALUATION			
1 Teezer (Greenside)	Easy			
An introductory sand game—hit through a tee stuck in the sand to get the tee to jump in the air.	Visualization			
	Control			
• Develops confidence in basic bunker swing mechanics. Develop your comfort level hitting into and through the sand. You learn to develop a consistent entry into the sand and understand how to use the club's bounce.	Confidence			
	Versatility			
	Swing Feel			

2 Line in the Sand (Greenside)	Easy
Hit balls out of a greenside bunker to a target without hitting a penalty line drawn in the sand. • Helps you develop control and learn consistent entry into the sand. Focuses on incorporating swing feel into your bunker play.	Visualization
	Control
	Confidence
	Versatility
	Swing Feel

3 A Day at the Beach (Greenside)	Moderate
Hit shots from a greenside bunker to a target on the green. • Develops your shot control and swing feel when hitting out of a greenside bunker. Instills confidence in thinking "up-and-down" when playing from a bunker.	Visualization
	Control
	Confidence
	Versatility
	Swing Feel

4 Around the Bend (Greenside)	Moderate
From a greenside bunker, you hit over a high face using different lofted clubs. • Helps you develop your skill and confidence to negotiate one of the most common bunker shots—elevating the ball out of a bunker. Enhances visualization and control of your club's loft and bounce, adding versatility to your game.	Visualization
	Control
	Confidence
	Versatility
	Swing Feel

5 Over the Dunes (Greenside)	Moderate
A competition where you hit out of the sand to different targets. • This multipurpose game adds competition to executing creative shots. It develops versatility making common bunker shots.	Visualization
	Control
	Confidence
	Versatility
	Swing Feel

6 Sandstar (Greenside)	Moderate				
One player throws three tees into a greenside bunker and all players play to targets on the green from where the tees land. • Develops your confidence in hitting out of a greenside bunker from a variety of locations.	Visualization				
	Control				
	Confidence				
	Versatility				
	Swing Feel				
7 Up and In (Greenside)	**Moderate**				
Compete to get ball up and down in the fewest strokes when pitching from a greenside bunker. • Develops your scoring skills. Helps broaden your swing mechanics and enhances transfer of these skills to the course.	Visualization				
	Control				
	Confidence				
	Versatility				
	Swing Feel				
8 Triple Play (Greenside)	**Moderate**				
Compete to get balls up and down from a greenside bunker in the fewest strokes, using different clubs for each shot. • Use your imagination and creativity when using different clubs for the same shot. Increases your proficiency with lofted clubs while creating real course situations.	Visualization				
	Control				
	Confidence				
	Versatility				
	Swing Feel				
9 Champ (Greenside)	**Difficult**				
A challenge competition where you earn letters to the word CHAMP for playing up-and-in out of a bunker. • Develops your ability to create shots, identify weaknesses in your technique, and increase your effectiveness in scoring in a competitive situation.	Visualization				
	Control				
	Confidence				
	Versatility				
	Swing Feel				

10 Bunker Match (Greenside)	Moderate				
A match play game where you compete against another player to win the most holes over a nine-hole course. • Develops your ability to play under pressure. Develops your swing feel as well as a sense of game management.	Visualization				
	Control				
	Confidence				
	Versatility				
	Swing Feel				
11 Pick Up Sticks (Greenside)	Difficult				
Similar to Sandstar, one player throws 3 tees in a greenside bunker and all players play to the green from the spots where the tees land. • Develops your ability to play under pressure from a variety of locations. Tests your shot-making ability and versatility.	Visualization				
	Control				
	Confidence				
	Versatility				
	Swing Feel				
12 Buried Alive (Greenside)	Difficult				
Compete to hit embedded balls out of a sand bunker to a target. • Helps you to identify what to expect and how to play successfully from a very difficult lie.	Visualization				
	Control				
	Confidence				
	Versatility				
	Swing Feel				

B. Fairway Bunker Games (3 Games)

Mastering fairway bunker shots also requires some initial instruction and coaching. There is a major difference between the two bunker shots:

- For most greenside bunker shots, you don't hit the ball, you let the sand carry the ball.
- For the fairway bunker, it is important to hit the ball before hitting the sand.

These games will give you the opportunity to practice this shot.

FAIRWAY BUNKER GAMES	EVALUATION			
13 Easy Out (Fairway)	**Easy**			
Hit short shots from a fairway bunker at a target 30 yards away. • Begin to develop mechanics required to make one of the tougher shots in golf. Gain confidence in the mechanics for this shot. Helps you transfer this scoring shot to the course.	Visualization			
	Control			
	Confidence			
	Versatility			
	Swing Feel			
14 Bunker Blast (Fairway)	**Moderate**			
Hit out of a fairway bunker and earn points by landing close to a target. • Hones your skill when making long bunker shots. By using different clubs, you become familiar with your options and gain confidence in this challenging stroke. Helps you transfer this scoring shot to the course.	Visualization			
	Control			
	Confidence			
	Versatility			
	Swing Feel			
15 Dealer's Choice (Fairway)	**Difficult**			
A challenge game where you must hit specific clubs out of a fairway bunker to a target. • Pushes the more accomplished player to new levels by putting a premium on successful bunker performance. Improves your creativity, versatility, and confidence in the swing mechanics needed to perform the long bunker shot under pressure.	Visualization			
	Control			
	Confidence			
	Versatility			
	Swing Feel			

BUNKER TIME

7
Take It to the Course

Nancy had trouble scoring her best in competition. Whenever she started to play well, she also started thinking that something was going to ruin the round: a bad shot, a three putt, a chunked chip. It could be anything to interrupt her concentration and hurt her score. She and Matt decided to play Worst Ball Scramble for nine holes to help her realize that she did not need to hit every shot perfectly to score well. They alternated this with Best Ball Scramble for nine holes. Nancy realized that she could recover from bad shots and get scores close to those she was getting with the Best Shot game. As her confidence grew, so did her scoring in competition.

This chapter is devoted to full swing games that can be played on the course.

Reading this chapter and playing the games in the *On The Course Booklet* will help you to:

- Transfer your practice shots to the course.
- Develop your confidence in using all of the clubs you use on the course.
- Get a better feel for how to handle competitive pressure.
- Enhance your versatility and creativity when getting out of trouble on the course.
- Have more fun while playing a round of golf.

Introduction: Take It to the Course

Now we get to take some games to the course! Here you can have fun while playing a full round of golf. There are two major benefits to playing these on-course games or taking some of the games from previous chapters and playing them on the course.

First, you get a chance to transfer what you have learned on the practice range to the course. This is a huge confidence builder.

Second, it is well-known that we perform skills best in the conditions where we learn and practice them.

Yet, most golfing practice takes place at a practice facility, not on the course. To increase the probability that your practice skills will transfer to regular golf rounds, devote some regular course time to practice. The best way to practice here is to play some of the games in the *On the Course* booklet—and track your progress.

Tech Talk: Playing on the Course

Master Professional Pat Lange has done an analysis to illustrate that a booming drive is not a prerequisite to a good score. She calculated the expected scoring averages for 18 holes on the typical golf course. It highlights the fact that *accuracy* from the fairway and on the green is the basis of lower scores.

This analysis is based on the assumption that no balls are hit poorly, there are no penalty strokes, and that the player averages two putts per green (see table).

Expected scores based on drive distances			
Drive distance from white tees	Average shots to green (18 holes)	Average number of putts (18 holes)	Total score
100 yards	61	36	97
125 yards	49	36	85
150 yards	41	36	77

For example, the first row in the table illustrates the expected score for a player who drives 100 yards from the white tees. If this player had no miss-hits, he/she would typically need 61 strokes to reach all the greens. With an average of two putts per green, this player would score 97 for 18 holes. The player who drives 125 yards would typically score 85! **The message: straight and dependable beats length and wild every time.**

Many players wonder about the ideal course length for their game. This is particularly true for courses with tees for all playing levels: championship, regular, senior, and women. If you want a challenging yet competitive round, especially when people in the group have different playing abilities, it is important to match the course yardage to your game.

Here's a rule-of-thumb: multiply the distance you typically hit your 5-iron by 36. This gives you the course yardage best-suited for your score against par. The table shows optimal course length based on this distance.

Given equal skill levels, a golfer who hits a 5-iron 130 yards can compete with a veteran player who hits the ball with the same club 190 yards. The shorter hitter would choose tee locations that make the course 4,680 yards long, and the longer-hitting player would choose tees that would make the same course 6,840 yards long (see table).

Optimal course length based on typical 5-iron distance	
Typical 5-iron distance (yards)	**Optimal course length (yards)**
100	3,600
110	3,960
120	4,320
130	4,680
140	5,040
150	5,400
160	5,760
170	6,120
180	6,480
190	6,840

On the Course (18 Games)

A couple of our on-the-course games are well-known standards. Many of you will know them if you have played in golf outings. We suggest some alternatives to make them more interesting. Several of them are designed for players of equal ability, so *beginning* players partnered with *experts* in these competitions would feel intimidated.

Reminder: when playing any of our games on the course, please keep other golfers in mind. Be considerate and do not slow up play.

GAME	EVALUATION				
1 Best Ball Scramble	**Easy**				
Each player hits from group's best shot off the tee. • This low-key game reduces the pressure of having to hit a successful tee shot. • It lowers the self-pressure you apply when you play with better golfers.	Visualization				
	Control				
	Confidence				
	Versatility				
	Swing Feel				
2 Tee Handicap	**Easy**				
Players are given additional chances to tee up in the fairway, based on their previous-hole performance. • Use this game when *beginners* are playing more experienced golfers. It gives *beginners* a sense of confidence as they develop their skill hitting from the tee and the grass.	Visualization				
	Control				
	Confidence				
	Versatility				
	Swing Feel				
3 Worst Ball Scramble	**Easy**				
Each player hits from the group's or player's worst shot. • This alternative to *Best Ball Scramble* gives you experience playing from difficult or poor positions. It helps you develop your catch-up game. This scramble variation helps you develop confidence when hitting out of trouble.	Visualization				
	Control				
	Confidence				
	Versatility				
	Swing Feel				

4 Muck It Up		**Moderate**		
Each player tries to hit the tee shot to a difficult position, and then challenges his/her opponent to play out the hole from this point. • This game has two goals: (1) it develops your ability to hit to targets, and (2) it makes you play trouble shots. It helps you to deal with adversity and learn to score from awkward locations.	Visualization			
	Control			
	Confidence			
	Versatility			
	Swing Feel			
5 Twenty-One		**Moderate**		
You earn points for hitting quality shots in addition to getting the lowest score. • Can be played by all levels as they improve their ability to execute shots. Hitting good shots is rewarded, giving you confidence as you can win points for hitting well.	Visualization			
	Control			
	Confidence			
	Versatility			
	Swing Feel			
6 Throw Me A Line		**Moderate**		
Players are given one foot of string for each handicap stroke. They can move the ball by measuring the distance with the string. Then this length is cut off and taken out of play. • This game helps less experienced players compete with more advanced players. It helps them develop more confidence while facing competitive pressure.	Visualization			
	Control			
	Confidence			
	Versatility			
	Swing Feel			
7 Rotation		**Moderate**		
Rotate through all clubs in your bag before using a club a second time. • Develop creativity, imagination, and new swing skills. It makes you adapt your swing to unusual situations and encourages you to plan ahead so you have the right club at the right time.	Visualization			
	Control			
	Confidence			
	Versatility			
	Swing Feel			

TAKE IT TO THE COURSE

8 Quarantine	Moderate				
A variation of Rotation, you quarantine one club in an opponent's bag after each hole. These clubs cannot be used until the quarantine is lifted. • Challenges your ability to play with each club in your bag. It helps you become a more versatile player.	Visualization				
	Control				
	Confidence				
	Versatility				
	Swing Feel				

9 Mix-Up	Moderate				
Limit your playing partners to certain clubs. • This game makes you determine which clubs you need for a hole and plan the proper strategy for scoring with them. Planning ahead is an integral part of successful golf. Strategy, imagination, and execution are all wrapped up in a nice little package in this game.	Visualization				
	Control				
	Confidence				
	Versatility				
	Swing Feel				

10 Limit	Moderate				
You have a limited number of clubs for each nine. • By limiting clubs, this game makes you plan ahead. Like *Mix-Up*, this game makes you rely on a variety of shots with a single club. It helps you develop imagination and versatility, and identify the difficulties you may have with certain shots.	Visualization				
	Control				
	Confidence				
	Versatility				
	Swing Feel				

11 Round Robin	Moderate				
In this variation of Limit you limit yourselves to a number of specific clubs for each nine. • Creates a competitive atmosphere where you can play to your strengths. It also helps you identify weaknesses in your game that may need to be developed. You learn more about your game by limiting the clubs to as few as possible.	Visualization				
	Control				
	Confidence				
	Versatility				
	Swing Feel				

12 Solo	Difficult				
You are limited to a single club for each hole. • Challenges your ability to execute a variety of shots with one club. It helps you develop an understanding of the swing mechanics required to make different shots using a single club.	Visualization				
	Control				
	Confidence				
	Versatility				
	Swing Feel				
13 Stretch	Easy				
Players choose a specific number of strokes and then play as usual until that limit is reached. • A a fun game and great confidence builder for golfers with equal skill.	Visualization				
	Control				
	Confidence				
	Versatility				
	Swing Feel				
14 Max-Min	Moderate				
Test your limits on the course by hitting one club lower and one club higher than you would normally choose for each shot. • Helps you develop confidence in making similar shots with a variety of clubs while playing on the course. It develop your versatility and confidence.	Visualization				
	Control				
	Confidence				
	Versatility				
	Swing Feel				
15 Bingo, Bango, Bongo	Easy				
A classic game in which players earn points for being first on the green, closest to the hole, and first to putt out. • This fun game gives players at all levels a chance to compete on equal footing. It helps develop confidence in approach shots, the short game, and putting.	Visualization				
	Control				
	Confidence				
	Versatility				
	Swing Feel				

TAKE IT TO THE COURSE

16 3-3-3	Difficult			
Sink a ball in three strokes or fewer, from three locations: your drive, an intermediate lie, and a greenside lie. • If played alone, this is a good game to help you diagnose your strengths on the course. Played competitively, it tests all your shot-making skills.	Visualization			
	Control			
	Confidence			
	Versatility			
	Swing Feel			
17 Adoption	Easy			
Players take turns choosing which of their playing partner's balls they want to hit for their next shot. • This relatively easy game gives weaker players confidence while having fun strategizing their approach to the course.	Visualization			
	Control			
	Confidence			
	Versatility			
	Swing Feel			
18 1-2-3-4	Easy to Difficult			
Players rotate through each of the playing partners' balls being played on a hole. • This is an excellent game for golfers at all levels and mixed group of golfers at different levels.	Visualization			
	Control			
	Confidence			
	Versatility			
	Swing Feel			

CHAPTER 7

8
Turning Your Game Around

The toughest thing in golf is to be honest with yourself. Don was a high school senior who came to Matt saying he wanted to get a golf scholarship at a Division I college. He wanted Matt to help him improve his game so he could do this.

When asked about his experience, it turned out that Don had developed an adequate swing but had never played in a tournament. While he stated that he played in the mid-80s, he had never developed an official handicap. He said he practiced about two hours a day at the municipal course where worked. When time permitted, he would play 18 holes of golf a couple of times a week. When asked about how he spent his practice time Don stated that he, "hit a couple of baskets of balls with his friends."

Matt told him that it was time to do a reality check by asking himself if he had time to commit to this improvement. Matt went on to explain to Don that he would have to devote himself to mental preparation, physical exercise, and expanding his shot and game skills. He would have to learn how to score under pressure and how to compete. Don had not considered these factors and reluctantly revised his goals to more modest expectations.

Reading this chapter will help you to:

- Understand the process you should go through to develop your golf game.
- Recognize what you need to do to learn, play, and practice better.

Rethinking Your Game

By now, you probably have played several of our games. You see how they can be effective in helping you groove your swing, but are only one part of the process you should follow for developing your overall golf game.

Building a balanced game requires an understanding of your general golfing goals. Why do you play golf?

- Is it for fun?
- Do you play for recreation or exercise?
- Is your primary reason for playing it because it offers opportunities to socialize or to cement business relationships?
- Is it a way to escape pressures of work or home?
- Or is it a way to engage in friendly competition?

Whatever your reasons, most people want to play better (or at least not so poorly that they embarrass themselves).

So, this leads us to the question, *"What are the worst ways to fully develop my golf game?"* Here are some, often used by well-meaning people:

- Limiting your development effort to hitting balls at a practice range. The problem here is that you tend to work on shots you're already most comfortable with. (For the testosterone crowd, driving range activity focuses more on crushing a ball as far as possible, with little attention to the finesse shots that will lower scores.)
- Rolling a dozen or so shots on the putting green before playing a round of golf.
- Thinking about developing their technique only when on the course.
- Devouring every golf swing tip and adjusting their stroke based on the latest magazine article or comments on TV.

If you are committed to playing better, then you have to step back and rethink how to go about it. We recommend that you follow these steps:

1. **Decide on the elements of your game that you want to enhance.** We offer in-depth self-assessments in *Swing Inventories* in the next chapter—these can give you valuable guidance. The swing inventories are highly focused to help you diagnose specific strengths and weaknesses with individual clubs and shots. They will help you identify how well the games are helping with specific golf swings.

2. **Set game improvement goals.** We give you specific ideas on how to make this decision in **Chapter 10**, *Goal-Setting*. We show how to analyze your game to identify areas you might want to develop. This is the information to give your teacher to get the most benefit from instruction.

3. **Go to a professional teacher who can help you develop your swing overall or fix specific elements that cause you problems.** This may be obvious, but the key here is *professional* teacher. In **Chapter 11,** *Learning How to Change Your Game,* we summarize the fundamental skill-learning principles that both players and teachers should know. This chapter also contains suggestions on what to look for in an effective teacher. While we wrote this chapter with *beginning* and *occasional* players in mind, it contains information important to all golfers who want to expand their golfing skills. It will help you understand what to expect from instruction and how to identify the best information sources for improving your game.

4. **Do not think that your game can be "fixed" with a one-hour lesson.** You will be disappointed! There is no way around it: you have to take what you learn from your teacher and practice it until it becomes automatic. Unfortunately, most golfers do not know how to practice effectively. So, **Chapter 12,** *Perfecting Your Practice,* describes the elements of effective practice and shows how to develop your personalized routine. Written for golfers at all levels, it shows why a well-constructed practice plan is important, and how to make the best use of your practice time. And of course we show how to integrate our games into your practice routine.

5. **Use a consistent approach to playing each shot.** Many players overlook this. We cover it in **Chapter 13**, *Getting Ready to Hit: The Pre-Shot Routine*. We provide you with advice on how to build your personal routine and give suggestions on how to focus your thoughts as you prepare to hit the ball. We wrote it with *occasional*, *skilled*, and *expert* players in mind, but the *beginning* player will benefit too, especially from the section on the psychology of the pre-shot routine. It can help all golfers understand why they may lack consistency from shot to shot.

6. **Understand your golfing emotions.** You and every other player has positive and negative thoughts that influence your behavior on the course. But embarrassment, frustration, stress, and anger over a poorly played shot can undermine a hole or round that had started with promise. Most of us have seen players implode after a series of poorly executed shots. It is a rare golfer who has not had the urge to turn a driver, 7-iron, or putter into a pretzel and hurl it into a nearby pond!

   In **Chapter 14,** *The Mental Game: Mind Over Swing*, we identify key elements of why and how our emotions influence our swings—an important chapter for players at all levels.

If you follow the steps above, you will give yourself every chance to improve your golf game. You will have the information needed to develop an automatic swing that you can rely on for all the standard golf shots. Once you have enhanced your swing through instruction and practice, you are ready to go to the course!

Evaluating Your Swing: Finding the Squeaky Wheel

Peggy, an advanced beginner, told Matt that she wanted to play golf better. She had been embarrassed at the last family golf outing, where she became so frustrated that she quit after the eleventh hole.

Matt asked what she meant by "better." Well, she wanted to hit the ball better so she did not look foolish when playing with her family. Matt probed: what did she mean by "hit the ball better"? Peggy got specific: she wanted to improve seven things, from driving through putting. "Which," Matt asked, "do you think is most important?"

Through this discussion, Peggy and Matt agreed on a few key goals and a specific plan for helping her develop her game. Through this process, Peggy understood that she could get better, but would have to do it over time, piece by piece. This renewed her interest in golf and gave her motivation and the confidence that she would not embarrass herself at the next outing.

Reading this chapter will help you to:

- Understand why it is important to diagnose your swing strengths and weaknesses.
- Learn how to diagnose your learning needs.

Identifying the Squeaky Wheel: What Do You Need to Fix?

Knowing what you have to do is the first step in improving your golf game. If you go to a coach without a sense of what is working and what is not, your coach will be limited in what to focus on.

Like Peggy in our story, you have to **identify specific areas of your game that need to be developed**. The more specifically you can identify them, the more likely it will be that you can fix them.

> "If You Don't Know Where You are Going, You'll Probably End Up Some Place Else"
>
> —Book by David Campbell

Be exact. It is easier for a teacher to focus on, "I need to improve the accuracy of my 50-yard wedge shot" than something general like, "I need to improve my short game." To fix your squeaky swing wheel, you need to know what is working and what isn't.

This chapter offers diagnostic self-evaluations that will help you to identify your specific golfing strengths and weaknesses. There are two groups: self-evaluations you can do at the practice range and those you can do while playing a round of golf. The key difference between the two is that the on-course records let you document your strengths and weaknesses while enjoying a round of golf.

All of these self-appraisals create a record you can show your teacher or coach, who can use them to help you with corrections to your swing and playing style.

Self-Evaluations at the Range

The best way to inventory your swing skills is to do a systematic evaluation at the range. Of course, you can do this while playing a round of golf—but you do not always hit all of your clubs over an 18-hole round, which leaves holes in your self-appraisal. You can also use them to chart your progress as your game improves.

The following self-assessments focus on your entire game, not just one or two shots. They include all of the shots covered in the games, from putting to full swing. You can do many of these self-evaluations as swing appraisals or play them as specialized games.

Note: We have included these self-evaluations in the *Practice and Performance Diary*.

Note: To minimize fatigue, be sure to spread these inventories over several practice sessions.

Putting Circle

The putt is one of the simplest golf strokes to do poorly. This is especially true when putting under the pressure of a competitive game. It is the only stroke where you have to consider all of the playing conditions to be successful—accounting for wind, rain, green conditions, distance, and slope. *Systematically evaluating your putting ability is one of the key self-evaluations you can do to identify your game improvement needs.*

The following evaluation is done in three series of four putts from 5 and 10 feet, followed by 15, 20, and 25-foot putts. It will help you diagnose any consistent putting errors you may make.

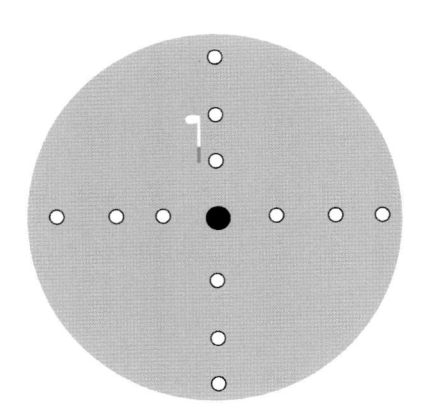

How to Play

1. Place 12 balls around a target cup. The closest should be approximately 5 feet away. Use your driver to estimate this distance.

2. Starting with the closest balls, putt each ball to the cup. Record the number of putts it takes to sink the ball. If you miss a putt, use the evaluation code to show the kind of miss (H, L, S, etc.—see example).

EVALUATING YOUR SWING: FINDING THE SQUEAKY WHEEL

In the example, the player completed the first series of short putts. He hit the hole in one stroke for the first two balls. (This is shown by the single *H*.) The third ball missed the hole to the right on the first stroke, and hit the hole on the second stroke. (The player recorded this as *R, H*.) The fourth ball hit the hole.

3. Do this two more times, once for the second and then third series. Then move on to the 10, 15, 20, and 25-foot putts.

PUTTING Circle Example

H = Hit	L = Left	S = Short
X = Miss-hit	R = Right	Lo = Long

Feet from pin	First Series — Ball				Second Series — Ball				Third Series — Ball			
	1	2	3	4	1	2	3	4	1	2	3	4
5'	H	H	R / H	H								
10'												
15'												
20'												
25'												

Notes and comments

Swing Inventory: Short Chips

Chips and pitches are skill shots that require a great deal of practice. The *skilled* player should be able to get the ball up and down in most situations. But *beginner* and *occasional* players may have less-demanding standards and will need more practice time for these shots.

That is the reason we provide so many games! It is important that you keep track of how well you chip and find the clubs you are most comfortable with for these score-lowering shots.

Chipping Circle

This self-evaluation is done in three series of four chips from 5, 10, 15, 20, and 25 yards from a target hole on the green.

How to Play

1. Place 4 balls at 3 locations around a target hole. Make each set about 5, 10, 15, 20 and 25 yards from target.

2. Starting with the 5-yard distance, chip 4 balls to target. Record distance and direction. In the example, the player hit first ball short (S) and to left (L). Second ball was straight to target but short (S). Third ball was short (S) but left (L), and fourth ball was left (L) and long (Lo).

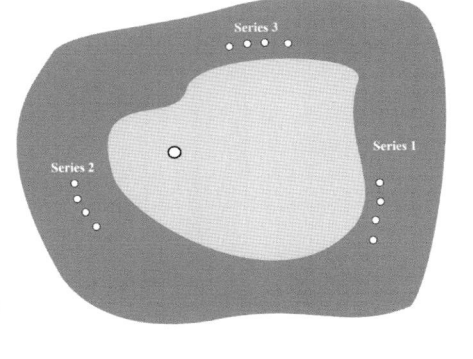

3. Do this for Second and Third series. Then move on to 10, 15, 20, and 25-yard chips.

4. We recommend that you do this evaluation with a variety of clubs so you get comfortable with a go-to club you can rely on.

CHIPPING Circle Example—Club Used								P Wedge			
H = Hit X = Miss-hit				L = Left R = Right				S = Short Lo = Long			
Feet from pin	First Series				Second Series				Third Series			
	Ball				Ball				Ball			
	1	2	3	4	1	2	3	4	1	2	3	4
5'	S L	S	S L	L Lo								
10'												
15'												
20'												
25'												

Notes and comments

Swing Inventory: Long Chips

We frequently make long chips to get out of trouble. This often happens when our tee shots go off the fairway and we must make a long shot under branches or some other obstruction to a landing area in the fairway. These shots call for both distance and directional control.

You should know how well you make these trouble shots—don't wait to try them on the course. Our inventory form below asks you to comment on each shot. This is information your teacher needs to help improve your game. (Additional forms are in the Appendix.)

How to Play

1. Take 6 balls, hit them to targets on the green and record the results of each shot. Hit (H) indicates that the ball stopped within approximately 3 club lengths of the target.

2. Start with the shortest distance and hit 6 balls. Then record any comments you have about the results. In the example, for 25 yards the player miss-hit (X) the first ball and hit the second ball to the right (R). The remaining 4 balls were either short (S) or long (L).

3. After the 25 yard series, move on to the longer shots.

4. We recommend that you do this evaluation with a variety of clubs. This helps you get a feel for how far each goes and helps you start to get comfortable with a go-to club you can rely on for these shots.

LONG CHIP Inventory—Club Used								
H = Hit X = Miss-hit				L = Left R = Right		S = Short Lo = Long		
Yards to Target	Ball						Comment
	1	2	3	4	5	6	
25	X	R	S	L	L	S	*Could not get a consistent feel for distance.*
50							
75							
100							

Swing Inventory: Pitching

This self-evaluation is done in three series over an obstacle from 10, 15, 25, 30, and 50 yards from a target.

How to Play

1. Place 4 balls behind an obstruction, like a bush or bunker. Alternatively, use a golf bag, umbrella, or chair.
2. Starting with the closest distance, pitch 4 balls to the nearest target hole.
3. Record the distance and direction. In the example, the player hit the first ball short and to the left (S,L). The second ball did not clear the obstruction (X). The third ball was short (S) but straight, and the fourth ball was short to the left (S,L).
4. Do this two more times from this distance for the second and third hole. Then move on to the 10, 15, 25, 30 and 50-yard pitches.
5. We recommend that you do this evaluation using a variety of clubs so you can get comfortable with a go-to club you can rely on.

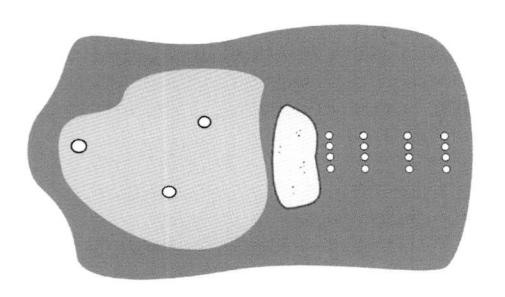

PITCHING Example —Club Used								*Sand Wedge*			
H = Hit X = Miss-hit				L = left R = Right				S = Short Lo = Long			
Yards from target	First Series				Second Series				Third Series			
	Ball				Ball				Ball			
	1	2	3	4	1	2	3	4	1	2	3	4
10	S L	X	S	S L								
15												
25												
30												
50												
Notes and comments												

Full Swing Inventory: Driving and Approach Shots

Most golfers overestimate how far they can hit a club and how accurate they are. This can be deadly for competitive players who want to score well. Since it is important to know the typical distance you can hit each club, we suggest that you do this self-assessment to evaluate both the quality of your stroke and the typical distance you hit the ball.

How to Play

1. Update the *Scoring Sheet* by indicating the clubs you use. For example, if you use a #4 rescue club instead of a 4-iron, write this in.

EVALUATING YOUR SWING: FINDING THE SQUEAKY WHEEL

2. Choose a club, hit 5 shots, and record the distance in the *Distance* column. Note any miss-hits (topped, behind the ball, etc.). Eliminate the longest and shortest shots. Your typical distance is the average of the remaining 4 shots. Move to a second club and hit five shots with it. Then return to the first club for 5 shots; finish with the second club for 5 shots.

3. Continue the evaluation using other clubs. To minimize fatigue, spread this self-assessment over several practice sessions. It is helpful to have another player, coach, or teacher assist with this evaluation. He or she could act as both a spotter who can confirm the distance each shot was hit.

4. If you want a complete self-evaluation, do this assessment from different fairway conditions, the rough, and uphill, sidehill, and downhill lies.

5. This form can also be used to evaluate your skill when hitting off the tee. The instructions are the same.

Full Swing Scoring Sheet

Club	Club used	1	2	3	4	5	6	7	8	9	10	Comment
Lob Wedge												
Sand Wedge												
Gap Wedge												
Pitching Wedge												
9-iron												
8-iron												
7-iron												
6-iron												
5-iron												
4-iron												
3-iron												
2-iron												
7-wood												
5-wood												
3-wood												
Driver												

Greenside Bunker Evaluation

As you work on perfecting greenside bunker shots, it is important to develop confidence in how far you can hit the ball using each of the lofted clubs when hitting with less than a full swing. As with other clubs, this is an area where an inventory of how well you can do is useful. This is essential to get a feel for your go-to club when hitting various distances from a bunker.

Bunker shots are made from a hazard that is filled with sand. This self-evaluation is done in three series from a bunker to a target 5, 10, 15, 20, and 25 yards away.

How to Play

1. Place 4 balls in a bunker with a consistent lie, either level, uphill, or downhill.

2. Start by hitting 4 balls to the closest target. Record distance and direction. In the example, the player hit first ball short and to left (S,L). Second ball did not clear lip (X). Third ball was short (S) but straight. Fourth ball stopped within a foot of target (H).

3. Repeat from this distance for second and third Series. Then move on to longer shots.

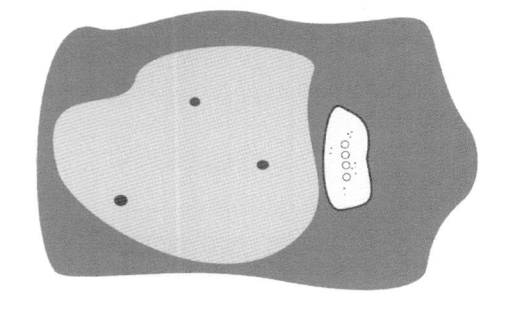

4. Since there is a variety of possible lies in bunker play, try this assessment from level, uphill, downhill, and embedded lies. In addition, the height of the bunker's face can vary from relatively low to high, so vary your evaluation to include lofted shots. Finally, do this evaluation in firm, damp and loose sand.

BUNKER Example —— Club Used								*S Wedge*			
H = Hit X = Miss-hit				L = left R = Right				S = Short Lo = Long			
Yards from pin	First Series				Second Series				Third Series			
	Ball				Ball				Ball			
	1	2	3	4	1	2	3	4	1	2	3	4
5	S L	X	S	H								
10												
15												
20												
25												
Notes and comments												

If you elect not to use any of the previous self-evaluations, we recommend any of the following on-course record-keeping plans to help you diagnose your overall game improvement needs.

Swing Inventory: On the Course

We recommend that you always keep track of your on-course performance beyond the number of strokes you make. This is true whether you are playing in a competitive tournament, friendly social game, or trying one of our games. Keeping track will help you focus on the elements of your game that are working, your go-to shots and clubs, and the ones that need extra work.

The best way to do this is to use either the *Basic Shot Tracking* or *Advanced Shot Tracking* forms we show below. If you are serious about developing your game, these records will help you monitor your performance and improvement over the golfing season.

All the shot tracking records in this book are important for your teacher/coach to review, since they give a good indication of your game's progress and what elements your coach can help you develop.

The first self-assessments are simple on-course shot recording techniques using a regular scorecard. This requires getting a separate scorecard to track of each of your shots while you play.

Basic Shot Tracking

There are many variations of this on-course record-keeping. Some players chart only fairways hit, greens hit in regulation, and number of putts. However, this abbreviated format does not list hits and misses in enough detail for you to identify what is working and where you need help.

The following example highlights this problem. For the first hole, the player did not hit the green in regulation—but you cannot tell what went wrong! What clubs were used to get to the green? Was it the wrong club or a bad shot? A week later, the player probably won't remember.

	Front Nine Example										
Hole	1	2	3	4	5	6	7	8	9	Score
Par	4	4	5	4	3	5	3	4	4	
Fairway	Y	N	N							
GIR	N	N	Y							
Putts	2	1	2							
Score	5	5	3							

If you are really interested in diagnosing your on-course play, we strongly recommend the *Advanced Shot Tracking* and *Thorough Shot Tracking* forms that come next.

Advanced Shot Tracking

A second self-evaluation option is to keep track of all of your shots on the course, using one of two simple techniques with a scorecard. For each hole, identify the club you used, the result of the shot (whether you hit your target—fairway, green, etc.), your score for the hole, and your evaluation of each shot.

Here's the benefit of this record-keeping: it not only helps you identify the clubs and shots that are working, it also helps you to see which clubs you don't use frequently. It gives you the opportunity to keep a thorough record of each round.

For the least complicated record-keeping: along the left side of a blank scorecard (where players' names normally go), use the following code to identify the typical shots you will be making during a round. (See the scorecard example that follows.)

D = Drive — Any shot from the tee box.

F = Fairway — A long shot from the fairway that you don't expect to hit the green.

A = Approach shot — A full-swing shot from the fairway that you want to hit the green.

S = Short Shot — Any pitch or chip to the green where you don't take a full swing.

Sn = Sand shot — Any shot from a bunker.

P = Putt — Any shot you roll to the hole.

Use the following code to identify the result of each shot:

H = Hit	I hit my target or expected landing zone.
L = Left	I was severely left of my target or landing zone.
R = Right	I was severely right of my target or landing zone.
S = Short	I was short of my target or landing zone.
Lo = Long	I was over my target or landing zone.
X = Miss-hit	I miss-hit the ball (topped, fat, shanked, etc.).

The first three holes on the sample scorecard illustrate how simple shot tracking works. These are highlighted with shading:

- For the first hole, the drive hit the fairway (H), and the approach shot was short (S), missing the green.
- The next short shot hit(H) the green and it took two putts (2) to finish the hole.
- The drive went right (R) at the second hole, followed by a short (S) approach shot.
- The short shot hit the green (H) and there was one putt (1) for a par.

	\multicolumn{9}{c	}{Hole}	
	1	2	3	4	5	6	7	8	9	Score
Par	4	4	5	4	3	5	3	4	4	
D	H	R	R							
F		S	H							
A	S		L							
S	H	H	H							
Sn										
P	2	1	2							
Score	5	4	6							

102 CHAPTER 9

Thorough Shot Tracking

A more thorough record using a scorecard is next. Here both the club used *and* the result were recorded. In this example:

- The player teed off on the first hole with the driver and hit the fairway *(D,H)*.
- The approach shot was a 7-iron that went right *(7,R)* into a bunker.
- The sand wedge was short of the hole *(Sw,S)*.
- It took two putts—the first was short *(P,S)*, and the second hit the hole *(P,H)*.

	\multicolumn{9}{c	}{Front Nine}	
Hole	1	2	3	4	5	6	7	8	9	**Score**
Par	4	4	5	4	3	5	3	4	4	
	D,H	D,R	D,R							
		H3,R	H4,R							
	7,R	8,H	6,R							
		Sw,S	PW,H							
	Sw, S									
	P,S P,H	P,L P,H	P,S P,S							
Score	5	6	6							

- The advantage of this format is clear. You or your teacher can review a scorecard like this a day or week later and see that many of the problems are hitting the longer clubs to the right, a problem that can be fixed.

If you choose to do these on-course self-evaluations, it's important to track several rounds, not just one. The reason is that we all have exceptional days—either world-class hitting or world-class duffing. Using one of these unusual rounds would be misleading. So, we suggest you record two or more rounds to get an accurate pattern of your swing strengths and weaknesses.

10
Goal-Setting:
What I Want to Get—How to Know If I'm Getting There

A beginning player came to Matt in March several years ago. She wanted to learn how to play golf, and her goal was to be able to beat her husband. Matt agreed to help (her husband's game was pretty bad.) Since her first goal was to learn basic golf, Matt took her onto the course and walked her through an easy hole—an hour that included many whiffs and wild swings. After this trial hole, Matt asked if she was still committed to her goal. She said, "This is harder than I expected. It looks so easy on TV!"

He reassured her that she had the basic ability, and as her skills improved, she would start to feel the game becoming easier. They put together simple objectives for each part of her game—for example, "Hit the ball every time you swing at it. Don't worry if it gets in the air or goes straight. Just hit it." They did the same for her short game and putting.

She practiced daily. They reset her goals many times over the next three months. When she started to show significant progress off the tee and putting, they spent more time on her short shots, breaking them down into simple objectives. By July she was breaking 100, and in August she shot 96—beating her husband by 6 shots!

Reading this chapter will help you to:

- Recognize why it is important to set goals if you want to improve your game.
- Know how to set clear expectations for your game.
- Begin to develop specific goals for enhancing your swing.
- Improve your ability to measure your personal progress.

Why Did You Buy This Book?

We'd like to think you got it so you could improve your game and have more fun playing! Indeed, we will help you with both. This book will help you, both on the range and on the course. But let us first look at why you go to a practice facility. There are many valid reasons to do so.

Home on the Range?

Do you go to the range to improve your game? You can go to a range, pound hundreds of balls, and hope that divine intervention grooves your perfect swing. *But, sorry—but just hitting a zillion balls at the range is unlikely to improve your game!* Curiously, our experience is that the majority of golfers expect this, but the sad reality is that you are more likely to overlearn any swing flaws you might have. (This approach reminds us of Barbara Sher's book, *I Could Do Anything If I Only Knew What It Was.*) You can go have a good time with friends while hitting balls, but improving your game takes help from an instructor—and our games in this book.

Do you go to the range to get ready for a round of golf? You want to stretch sleeping muscles and get reacquainted with the feel of a successful swing. This is "purposeful rehearsal," very helpful. To get the most from this warm-up, hit a variety of clubs and hit each with some target in mind. And playing one or more of our games will help you find the focus you will need on the course.

Do you go to maintain a well-learned swing? Many experienced golfers do this. Professional golfers spend hours hitting balls to keep their well-honed skill sharp. The internationally acclaimed concert pianist Jan Paderewski said, "If I miss one day of practice, I notice it. If I miss two days, the critics notice it. If I miss three days, the audience notices it." The applies to your golf swing—use it or lose it. Many of our games give advanced golfers the opportunity to maintain skill while having fun.

Do you go to improve your swing? Again, don't just go hit a bunch of balls—it won't work. This is one of the reasons we wrote this book, to help you *thoughtfully practice for improvement*. If this is your plan, follow these four steps:

1. *Identify what aspects of your game need to improve.* We showed ways to do this in Chapter 9, *Evaluating Your Swing: Finding the Squeaky Wheel.*

2. *Build realistic improvement goals and expectations for fixing them.* That's in this chapter.

3. *Get competent instruction.* This is covered in Chapter 11, *Learning How to Change Your Game.*

4. *Integrate this advice into your game through effective practice (Chapter 12, Perfecting Your Practice)* and by playing our games.

If you follow these steps, you will be ready to take your improved game to the course.

Goals and Expectations

A ***goal*** is a specific thing you want to accomplish within a specific timeframe.

An ***expectation*** is the realistic probability that you can accomplish the goal.

These two are closely related.

In golf, some goals are realistic and some are wishful thinking. If your goal is to qualify for the British Open, that is admirable, but your expectation that this is possible is the test that tells whether your goal is achievable. For most of us, this one is out of reach and does not match reality. In golf, your expectations depend on a variety of factors. We will highlight some of these next.

Let's suppose that you have the goal of breaking 85 three times before the end of the current golf season. Is that realistic? Here's a four-step reality check:

Step 1 in your reality check is to look at your playing level. If you currently are shooting in the low 90s, then 85 might be a realistic expectation. But if your score is consistently over 100, then your expectation might be a stretch.

Step 2 is to decide how much time you're willing to put into achieving your goal. If you need to trim many shots off your game and are willing to practice 10 hours a week and take weekly lessons, then your expectations are realistic. But if your practice is limited to hitting a small bucket of balls at the driving range every other week, your goal is less practical.

Step 3 is to examine your fitness level. Keeping yourself in good physical shape will help you to strike the ball more consistently.

Step 4 is to factor in the amount of on-course playing time you expect. The more time you spend on the course, the more likely you are to achieve your goals by translating your practice into play.

Expectations play an immense role in your enjoyment of your game. As in everything else in life, **unrealistic expectations lead to frustration, and frustration is a wooden stake in the heart of your game.** More golf clubs are bent, twisted, tossed, and drowned due to frustration than any other plague on the links. For the *beginning* player, the disappointment that comes from unrealistic expectations frequently leads to abandoning the game altogether, a very sad loss. Instead, realistic goals—those that you can reasonably meet—actually *motivate* advancing your game. As you stretch yourself to meet them, your motivation level and confidence increase.

Let's take the case of Pat Niblick. Pat wants to have more fun and improve his game. Pat is a typical weekend golfer and has been routinely shooting in the lower 90s, bogey golf, and wants to break 85 routinely. Pat completed the on-course self-assessment for three rounds and summarized his results in the table on the following page.

Putting	One Putt	14
	Two Putts	17
	Three Putts	20
	Four putts	3
Greens in Regulation	Hit	7
	Short	18
	Right	12
	Left	10
	Long	7
Fairways	Hit	16
	Right	13
	Left	9

Once Pat completed this relatively simple analysis he realized that he could identify specific areas for improvement.

Looking at his putting summary, Pat realized that reducing the number of three-putts and four-putts from an average of 7 per round to 3 per round could reduce his score by 4 strokes. Pat also noticed that he could reduce his score further by hitting the green in regulation more frequently.

Pat now had something specific to focus on to improve his game. He could realistically establish a game improvement plan with the goals of increasing his putting accuracy and the number of greens hit in regulation.

Setting Your Goals

Many people make personal resolutions: stop smoking, lose weight, save for retirement. The problem with most of these is that they are too general. They are not flawed in concept, but they are flawed by being unfocused. **Here is how to set golfing goals that you have every chance of meeting:**

1. *Make your goal* **specific**. Deciding to "lower my scores from the mid-90s to 85 and lower" is not a specific goal—it is a broad outcome. Outcomes are the consequence of having achieved one of more specific playing goals. To be specific, your goal must identify targeted skills. Looking back at Pat's self-assessment, it is clear that reducing

the number of three and four putts and hitting more greens in regulation will help Pat achieve the outcome. So, Pat set one goal: "To reduce the number of four and three putts per round to three or fewer."

2. *Make your goal* **measurable**. Pat could have said that he wanted to "improve his game." This is not a statement that is measurable. "Improve" has too many interpretations. It could mean fewer strokes per round. It could also mean fewer lost balls or fewer clubs in the pond. "three or fewer four and three-putts per round" can be counted, and is a measurable goal.

3. *Give your goal a specific* **deadline.** A deadline is a specific time when the goal will be achieved. It should be as specific as the goal. Stating "I will get more organized" is not specific in either the goal or timeframe. For procrastinators and wishful thinkers, this could mean tomorrow, next week, or next month. A more precise goal for Pat would be, "I will reduce the number of three-putts and four-putts per round to 3 or fewer before the Club Championship on August 23." Note the specific deadline.

4. *Your goal needs a* **specific benefit to you** *to motivate you to achieve it.* Pat has set his putting goal as "I will reduce the number of three-putts and four-putts per round to 3 or fewer before the Club Championship on August 23, so I can place in the top five in my flight."

5. *Your goal must be* **achievable (realistic).** If Pat sets the goal in early May, he may meet it. On the other hand, if Pat sets it on the first of August, the goal is less realistic; the expectation does not match reality. Several factors decide whether a goal is achievable. Being achievable depends on your expectations and the reality of your goal. The best way to determine if a goal is achievable is to develop a personal plan.

How To Get There: Developing a Personal Plan

Pat's personal plan is shown in the *Personal Planning Guide* that follows. This guide documents the steps to achieving a specific goal. Importantly, it also identifies the benefits to Pat of achieving it. This is the WIIFM (*What's In It For Me?*). If Pat puts sufficient effort into accomplishing his goal, there should be a payoff—his WIIFM.

Goal. Pat has completed the first section of this form with his goal: "Reduce the number of three-putts and four-putts per round to 3 or fewer before the club championship on August 23, to give me a shot at being the top five in my flight."

Benefits. The next section shows what Pat will get from achieving this goal—being more competitive..

How Will I Get There? We suggested that Pat complete this section with the help of his coach, the person who will give Pat the insight needed to improve his swing. *How Will I Get There?* details specific steps needed to reach his goal. These steps should be as detailed as the goal. The benefit of specific steps is that it can be reinforcing to check them off when they are completed. In addition, if Pat is completing these steps and is not getting any closer to the goal, it indicates a flaw in one or more of the steps.

What Do I Need to Get There? Here Pat lists the resources he needs to implement his plan successfully. Listing resources may seem obvious, but the time spent here is critical: it makes Pat make a reality check to have confidence that his goal is achievable. For example, if Pat recognized that he needed six lessons at $85 apiece ($510) but could only afford $400 for lessons, balls, and greens fees, he would have to rethink his plan.

Possible Obstacles and Solutions. This is another reality check. Obstacles are the barriers and landmines that can derail achieving your goal. Some obstacles can be overcome, but some are insurmountable. For example, if Pat plans to play 18 holes weekly starting in December and he lives in Maine, the weather would be an insurmountable obstacle. Most obstacles can be dealt with if one is flexible and creative. This is another opportunity to get advice from someone familiar with the situation.

How Can I Track My Progress? Who Will Help Me? Private goals frequently evaporate. Think of the number of New Year's resolutions you have made. If you didn't make them public, then it's unlikely you made any progress toward achieving them. Making a public commitment to a goal enhances the probability that it will be met. Involving a friend, coach, or playing partner is one way to publically commit to a goal. Some people even have the playing partners sign or initial their guides. Pat enlisted his teacher, Fran Mashie, and playing partner, Bob Brassie, to help him track his progress.

Pat could set up an additional goal sheet, one for developing more accuracy in hitting the green. In fact, it is wise to consider several aspects of the game that could be improved. But it is *not* a good idea to have more than three game improvement goals at a time. The reason is simple. Changing a swing takes time, practice, and requires conscious attention until it becomes automatic. Having too many thoughts while playing interferes with the automatic nature of the swing.

PERSONAL PLANNING GUIDE

GOAL (What I want to achieve)

Reduce the number of three-putts and four-putts per round to 3 or fewer before the club championship on August 23, to give me a shot at being the top five in my flight.

BENEFITS (What I will get from achieving this goal)

1.	*Play a more competitive game for the championship; get to the top five.*
2.	*Develop my overall golf game.*

HOW WILL I GET THERE? (Steps to achieve this goal)

	Action Steps	Target Dates
1.	*Get a putting lesson from Fran Mashie*	*Next week*
2.	*Practice putting twice a week after the lesson*	
3.	*Play 27 holes of golf a week*	
4.	*Play the games that Fran recommends*	*Weekly*

WHAT DO I NEED TO GET THERE? (Time, Material, Money, Information)

Time	Budget time for an additional nine holes per week
Material	101 Games for Golf book
Money	Need $85 per lesson
Information	Lessons from Fran

POSSIBLE OBSTACLES (What could interfere with achieving this goal)

1.	Outer Banks vacation for two weeks in July; can I practice there?
2.	Fran's suggestions may not work for me.

POSSIBLE SOLUTIONS TO OBSTACLES (Ways to get around obstacles)

1.	Check for golf courses, practice greens, and fees in the area.
2.	Follow up with Fran or get advice from another coach.

HOW CAN I TRACK MY PROGRESS? (How will I know I am reaching this goal?)

1.	Use the simple On Course idea to keep a running record of my putts until August.
2.	

WHO WILL HELP ME TRACK MY PROGRESS?

1.	Fran Mashie for technique
2.	Bob Brassie for commitment and on-course play.

IS THIS GOAL WORTH THE TIME, EFFORT, MONEY, AND TRAINING?

YES: __X__   NO: _____   YES, BUT LATER: _____

Eat the Elephant One Bite at a Time

Finally, it is important to remember the old story about the villager who was given the task of eating an elephant. When asked about how it is possible for one small person to consume the gigantic meal he was told, "*Do it one bite at a time.*" This is the approach you should take when developing your golf game. Do it one swing at a time. Be realistic and bring your expectations in line with what you can do.

11
Learning How to Change Your Game

Matt met a middle-aged man at a party who asked him what he should look for in a golf teacher. He was disappointed with his current teacher but was reluctant to change. Matt paused then said, "Find the teacher who has the versatility and the resources to make you as good as you want to be. One of the keys is to find a teacher who is still learning. This will let you know that he or she still has the desire to be the best."

We challenge you golfers who want to learn to never stop seeking a great teacher. A great teacher is informed on every aspect of golf from swing science, to mechanics, to nutrition. Good luck! (If we had read this chapter long ago, we would have improved much sooner.)

Reading this chapter will help you to:

- Know what is meant by muscle memory.
- Understand the three stages of skill learning.
- Realize the impact a new swing will have on your game.
- Know where to go for advice on improving your golf game.
- Recognize what to look for in a golf coach or teacher.

Introduction: How We Learn

Have you ever watched a good golfer hit an effortless shot and wonder how the person did that? Have you ever hit the perfect shot in a lesson only to find out a week later that you could not perform that shot again? Have you ever found that a shot you had hit successfully when practicing took a vacation on the course?

If you have faced any of these situations then this chapter will help you understand why this can happen and what you can do about it.

Before we begin we want to cover some of the key elements of how we learn a new skill. You need to understand them if you want to know how you can learn most effectively.

Tech Talk: Skill Learning and Muscle Memory

The term "muscle memory" is another term for what psychologists call motor memory. Both refer to the relatively permanent learning of some physical activity. It is the ability to recall the feeling of a successful activity. This accounts for the fact that people with amnesia can still perform daily activities such as walking, brushing their teeth, and golfing. (Amnesia does not apply to the situation where someone fails to recall the muffed shot out of the rough when reporting a golf score.) For clarity, we will refer to the specialized movements needed to swing the golf club as *"swing mechanics"*—the physical actions needed to hit a golf ball successfully. Learning this skill is a systematic process that we describe in this Tech Talk.

The Learning Process

There are three steps in learning. The first is called **Acquisition.** This is where we initially learn new golfing ideas or swing mechanics. For most golfers this comes from a teacher or coach. Others get it by reading instructional books, watching TV, or receiving advice from friends. Still others attempt to learn golf by grabbing a club and thrashing around until they eventually hit the ball. We will discuss effective *acquisition* techniques later in this chapter.

> Hitting a golf ball correctly is the most sophisticated and complicated maneuver in all of sport with the possible exception of eating a hot dog at a ball game without getting mustard on your shirt.
>
> —Ray Fitzgerald

Once we learn something we have to save it somewhere. This is called **Retention.** It is the process of storing the information or skill you are learning and making it available for use later. Written material is retained through rehearsal and memorization. **Skills like golf are retained through physical practice**. Being able to recite the correct motions for a golf swing in no way relates to the ability to perform it. This highlights the problem with trying to learn golf from books and TV. Seeing is not doing. Golfers encounter this every day. One playing partner recites all of the textbook rules for the proper stance while topping the ball twenty yards. Another person slices a ball into the Swamp of Despond and then offers up a litany of all of the swing mistakes that he made.

When you say, *"I hit the ball well in practice, why can't I do the same on the course?"* This is a problem with the third stage of learning, **Transfer**, taking what was learned in a lesson or developed in the practice area to the course. One reason that this happens is because **the learning and practice environments are not the same as the course environment**. There are major physical and mental differences between the two. Some key differences are:

1. The mental and emotional environment in the practice area is different than that found on the course. The key change is that the feeling of pressure to perform and/or compete is lacking on the range. As we pointed out in Chapter 1, unless you shank a ball into someone's car in the parking lot, there are no consequences for poor shots on the practice range. When you **Practice with Consequence** by being rewarded for good shots and penalized for poor shots you are more likely to duplicate the playing atmosphere found on the course. Each of our games does this by putting you in a simple competition where good shots are reinforced and poor shots make you lose points.

2. The practice area does not duplicate the physical conditions you experience on the golf course. Practice ranges are flat and manicured to duplicate perfect fairway conditions, not the rough. There are no trees, bushes, and rocks to navigate, and most practice ranges do not have fairway bunkers to escape.

3. When practicing we typically don't rotate through the progression of shots and lies we would normally find on the course. On the course we rarely hit the same club ten times in a row. We cycle through a variety of clubs.

4. The plastic mats found on many driving ranges do not have the feel of hitting from grass. They are more forgiving, not to mention the fact that they leave nasty green stripes on your golf clubs. In addition, the balls found on most practice facilities are much different than those you would use in day-to-day play. The typical range ball is a cement-like composite designed to last forever. It does not have the feel or flight characteristics of the balls you hit when playing.

One key element to successful transfer is to make the learning environment as similar to the game environment as possible. Ideally, all practice sessions would take place on a golf course, but this is not possible. Our games move closer to the course environment by encouraging you to play a variety of shots using a variety of clubs. Since the games have a low level of competition built in they can simulate the friendly rivalry found on the course. The key is to **practice the way you play so you will play the way you practice.**

Learning Pieces: Part vs. Whole Learning

When Dennis learned how to swim his grandfather took him to the pool and taught him how to float. He showed him that he could do this with his face in the water and how to raise his head to breathe. Then he learned to kick across the pool lying on a small, inflatable raft. Soon after this Dennis found out that his arms could paddle. Eventually, he put all of the pieces together and learned to doggy paddle: his first independent stroke. Dennis learned how to swim by learning pieces and then 'pasting' them together. This is called **part learning.**

Part learning is the best approach for *Beginners*. Here is another example. When Dennis taught his daughter to drive a stick shift, he broke the initial sessions into locating and depressing the clutch, shifting from gear to gear, slowly releasing the clutch while pressing on the accelerator, shifting the gears while moving, starting the car in first gear without stalling and finally, stopping the car in first gear without stalling. All of the elements were learned and practiced separately. Then they were integrated into the whole driving process of starting, shifting gears, driving, and stopping without stalling the car. Golf drills are part learning. They break the swing into pieces. Each piece is practiced independently with the expectation that the swing skills developed in the drill will be incorporated into the full swing.

The other approach to learning a complex skill is to try to do the whole thing at once. This is **whole learning**. This is similar to the process that happens when a person who is skilled with a stick shift sedan moves to a new car with a different shift pattern. It can be learned all at once without breaking the sequence into pieces. In golf, this would be teaching a competent bunker player how to hit a ball embedded in a downhill lie in a greenside bunker. This shot could be taught and practiced all at once.

The key point is that ***Beginners* learn best from part learning**; starting with the pieces and then assembling them into the full swing. **Accomplished players learn best from whole learning**. They can see or be told about a new shot and then quickly incorporate this into their full swing.

Learning Strategies

Unless you are a purely social golfer who is satisfied with your game, most of us want to improve at golf. There are two strategies your teacher could take to help you. One of these is to totally rebuild your swing by making major alterations to the set up, take away, hand position, weight shift, and shoulder rotation, etc. This is a pretty massive change. We call this a **revolutionary approach**. This approach works for the golfer whose basic swing limits his or her overall ability to improve.

A second approach is to make small changes in a swing. This might be changing from a weak to stronger grip with a driver, learning to keep the hands ahead of the club face when chipping, or keeping the head still when putting. These small changes can either improve a game immediately or they can build up to develop an enhanced swing. We call these **evolutionary changes**, small adjustments that improve the swing over time. Most modifications that our instructors make fall somewhere between evolutionary and revolutionary.

"I rebuilt my swing. My shots are better, but my scores are worse!"

Golfers who make major, revolutionary swing changes have this problem. They spend time and money taking lessons and have made major swing changes. To their dismay, their scores increase although they may be hitting the ball better. This is because new swing habits require conscious thought. Their swing is no longer automatic. **The body has not fully integrated the new swing and thinking gets in the way of an Unconsciously Skilled shot**.

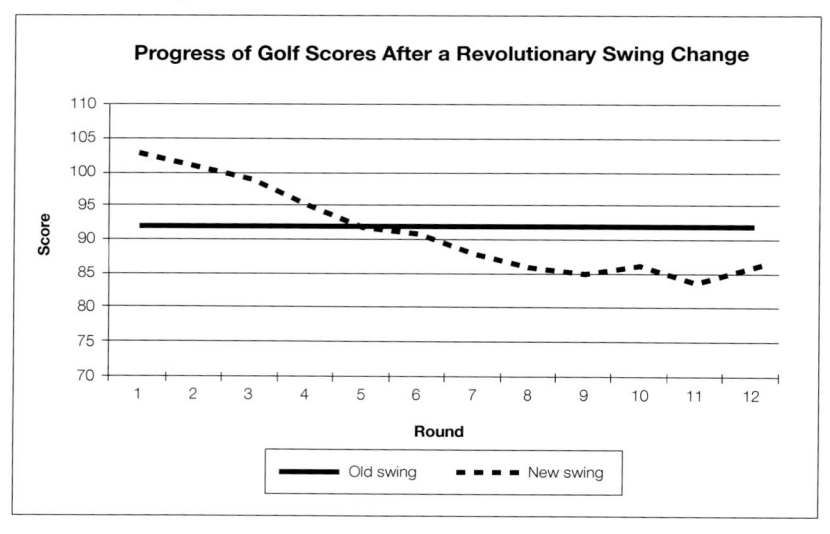

Progress of Golf Scores After a Revolutionary Swing Change

This figure illustrates what can happen when you change from a mediocre swing to a better one after a major (revolutionary) swing change. The solid line shows the scores ranging in the lower 90s representing the typical score with the old swing.

So the player goes to a teacher who makes fundamental changes in the golfer's swing. Initially the scores increase, as shown in the first four rounds with the dotted line. After practicing the new swing, the golfer's scores start to drop as the swing becomes more automatic. There are several reasons for this trend:

1. In the first weeks following the change, the new swing is not automatic. This is especially true if the new swing has not been practiced efficiently. In fact, unless you really focus on the changes, **elements of the new and old swing start to interfere with each other—** creating miss-hits. What happens is that there are too many swing thoughts, the old ones and the new ones. With a new swing you are more likely to integrate new swing thoughts into your pre-shot routine without discarding the old ones. This causes confusion. The overabundance of ideas can distract from the mechanics of what was once a routine shot. As you replace the old thoughts with the correct ones, this uncertainty fades and the new swing becomes more automatic.

2. When the miss-hits happen you lose confidence in your new stroke. **Confidence in the swing is fundamental to good golf**. Successful practice will enhance confidence. Most of our games will help you establish trust in your swing. Playing some of the games in the booklet *On the Course*, will help you to cement these new swing patterns and encourage transfer to the course. Ask your teacher which ones will help the most.

3. When the new swing becomes automatic, you have to rethink your shot selection and course management. For example, if you are a player who used to hit a 7-iron 135 yards and now you hit it 145 yards, you must rethink how to play the 140 yard par-three hole.

It is almost **inevitable that scores will become unstable until swing changes become automatic**. The message here is twofold. First, be patient! Your game will improve as you become confident in the altered swing. The second is practice. Road testing a new swing only on the course is a bad idea if you want to improve your scores but is a basic requirement if you want to transfer your new skills to your play.

In Chapter 12 we give you recommendations on how you can develop a practice routine that will speed the integration of your new swing into your game on the course. Of course, our games will give you the necessary quality preparation you need to increase your confidence and take the swing to the course successfully.

If It's Bent or Broke, How to Fix It

There is an old saying, "A person who acts as his own attorney has a fool for a client." The same could be said for the player who attempts to teach himself golf. You can find dozens of books, films, tapes, and TV programs that provide game improvement advice.

Spending an afternoon watching the Golf Channel might persuade you that the latest club, swing device, exercise machine, or dietary supplement will transform you into a par golfer.

> A Dog with no master learns few tricks.
>
> —Benjamin Franklin

While many of these aids, tips, and drills can help, we must rely on Scotland's national poet, Robert Burns, who wrote, "Oh would some power the giftie gie us, to see ourselves as others see us." The best way to learn golf is to get a competent teacher to observe, diagnose, and advise to help you develop your swing and correct your flaws.

Group vs. Individual Instruction

Basically, there are two ways you can learn golf with guidance from a trained professional. The first is through a group lesson; the second is through individual instruction. Below are some of the pros and cons of each.

Group Instruction (Method vs. Tailored)

Group instruction can take place through famous name golf schools or through local instructional facilities. The least effective form of group instruction involves a show-and-tell format. In this format the teacher will spend an hour or two discussing and demonstrating elements of the swing and talking about fixes for problems. The benefit of this over watching golf instruction on television or reading about it in a book or magazine is that there are opportunities for question and answer. The major drawback is that you don't have an opportunity to hold a club, swing it, and get feedback. Learning by seeing is not an effective way to improve your game. A second drawback is that you don't get individualized instruction or attention.

More effective group instruction occurs in golf schools that give you the opportunity to swing the club. These courses can last from two to four consecutive days of instruction and opportunities to play. Local schools frequently space their class times over several weeks. The better schools have limited class size so there is opportunity for individualized instruction, but keep in mind, you are in a class, so much of the work is group work. In addition, the better schools have competent, well qualified teachers with both an expertise in teaching and a broad range of golf skills.

The benefit of golf schools is that they provide you with instruction on specific elements of the game: putting, chipping, pitching, etc. Usually this is done in three to four hour morning sessions with opportunities to take this instruction to a course in the afternoon. The focused teaching model in these courses can lead to quick initial learning. Another benefit is that the cost per teaching hour is less than you would find with the same amount of time in private lessons. The better schools will give you a personalized workbook with observations and recommendations, drills, and practice suggestions. Some will even provide you with a personalized video to refer to when the school is over.

A danger of the intensive, short-term training you get in a golf school is that it is essentially a form of massed instruction and practice. Unless the new skills you acquire in the school are practiced effectively, they will be lost quickly. (The next chapter covers effective practice techniques in more detail.)

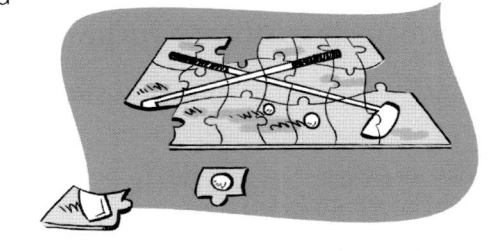

A second potential danger, especially for the novice golfer, is that you can become overloaded with new information. We recommend that the *beginner* look for group instruction that is spread over several weeks or months rather than being fit into a long weekend. A final issue with the school model is that you don't get continuity, the opportunity to discuss problems with a teacher who is familiar with you, your game, and your goals over an extended period of time. This is something you can get only from a teacher who will give you private lessons.

If you do decide to consider a golf school, here are things to consider:

- **Breadth of instruction.** Some schools cover all aspects of golf, others focus on specific elements such as the short game or physical conditioning. Your choice should be consistent with your development goals.
- **Cost.** While the school will clearly tell you the direct cost of instruction there will be hidden costs. Some of the other expenses would be travel, dining and lodging, gratuities, etc. Be sure to factor these expenses into your plans.
- **Student:Teacher ratio.** The smaller this ratio is the better. While it would be great if this was 1:1, a larger ratio should be expected.
- **Instruction and playing time.** You are paying for instruction time so you want as much instruction as possible. To what extent will the program address your specific learning needs and goals? Does the coaching include only range teaching or does in include playing instruction? Is there time for you to practice the skills you are learning both on the range and on a course?
- **Teaching staff qualifications.** Does the staff consist of PGA teaching professionals?
- **Instructional method.** Does the school advocate one specific method or does it tailor the instruction to your needs?
- **Teaching technology.** Does the program have up-to-date technology that can help to diagnose and illustrate your swing?
- **Follow-up services.** Will you be given personalized suggestions and recommendations to take home? Is there an opportunity for follow-up calls or contacts to clarify issues that were not clear when you left?

Individual Instruction

There are many factors to consider when selecting an individual golfing instructor. Are you a social player or are you planning to play competitively?

What is your current skill level? Are you planning to make a long-term commitment or do you expect to take intermittent lessons?

It may seem that the best teacher is someone who is an expert golfer. This is not necessarily the case. While being good at golf is a prerequisite for being a good teacher, it does not guarantee that the person has the talent to teach. There is a wide variety of people willing to tell you how to swing a golf club. Here are some of the types of teachers you will find and the level of instruction you will probably find from each.

Family member or friend who is an *occasional* golfer—This person is usually an eager weekend golfer who will spend time showing you swing basics as he or she understands them. Unless this person is trained as a teacher and has a comprehensive understanding of various swing flaws and how to identify and fix them, he or she is unlikely to advance your skill much beyond the *beginner* level.

Family member or friend who is a skilled player—This person is a skilled or expert golfer who has a good understanding of the game but who has no specific training in how to diagnose swing flaws, teach, and guide your game. This person may give good advice but it may not be the suggestions that fit your specific game. Finally, he or she may not be knowledgeable enough to teach all aspects of the game.

PGA and LPGA Professional—The PGA and LPGA professional has been tested and evaluated by his or her peers to obtain a specific professional classification. There is a variety of PGA professionals. Some have expertise in club fitting, some have training in golf course design and maintenance, and others have certificates in golf club management. A Master Teaching Professional is an individual who has had years of teaching experience and training and who has demonstrated exemplary skill in *teaching golf*. This person has successfully completed a specialized training program that focuses on all aspects of the golf game. You can expect these teachers to provide top-level instruction.

Other Teaching Professionals—A number of organizations train and certify golfers as professional teachers. Frequently these teachers hold certificates but are not necessarily certified as PGA or LPGA professionals. Examples of this kind of teacher would be the person who works with a famous teaching school and who is certified as an instructor by that school or who has completed a training course offered by an instructional school. Another example is a person who has been certified as a Golf Teaching Professional by the USGTF.

What to Look for in a Golf Teacher

In addition to the background, training, and certification, here are some other qualities to look for in a teacher:

Background and experience—Does the person have the training and expertise to provide you with competent advice? One way to determine this is to ask about the person's credentials. Another approach would be to ask other students about their impressions. If you plan to play competitively you should ask about the persons experience in collegiate and PGA sponsored tournaments.

Personal touch, connection and rapport—Is the person genuinely interested in you and helping you improve your game? Is the person a good listener and does he/she give you his/her full attention? Does the person question more than tell? In the first meeting, he or she should get a full understanding of your experience, goals, expertise, and plans. On the other side, do you feel a sense of comfort with the person? It is important that there be both a personal and professional connection between you and your teacher.

Fred 9 to 5

By Herb Kurtzberg

Tailored approach—Will the person help you find the best stroke for you or does the person have a fixed model and attempt to fit you into that model? The better coach will understand the essentials of the successful golf swing and will tailor the swing to your athleticism, size, interests, equipment, and ability. Unless you have to make a radical change to your swing, you should be able to see rapid improvement.

Setting realistic expectations—Will the person help you set realistic expectations by telling you what your lesson plan will be, and how long it will take to get results? Beware of the person who promises to fix a problem instantly. While you should see progress after one lesson, making a swing permanent takes practice. Quick fixes are no more reliable than the weight loss products seen in infomercials. The competent coach should evaluate your swing and work on the fundamentals. Using the goal setting sheet we describe in Chapter 10 can help you and your coach set realistic expectations as to what can and cannot be accomplished.

> Be honest with yourself. What you would find out in six months of practice [alone], your pro can tell you in five minutes.
>
> —Harvey Penick

Time and money—Is the person candid about fees and payment? Does the person also let you know his/her availability and the amount of time he/she can commit to helping you? Does the person have a variety of teaching options/programs that can fit your budget and learning goals? This can include individual or group lessons, supervised practice sessions, and/or playing lessons.

Compatible teaching style—Is the person's teaching style compatible with your learning style? Some people learn by seeing, others learn by hearing, still others learn by doing first. Does the instructor adjust to teach in a way the meets your personal style? Peter Block, in his book *Flawless Consulting,* writes about different consulting styles. These fall onto a continuum. At one extreme is the "Expert" approach. People following this approach tell the client what has to be done. At the opposite extreme is the "Pair-of-Hands" approach. This person asks you what needs to be done and then does exactly what you want. Neither of these approaches is perfect. The ideal teachers have has a balance between the expert and pair-of-hands models. They are flexible to find out what you want but candid enough to say honestly what you have to do to get there.

Working with children—Does the person have experience with children? Can the person establish rapport with the child? Is there a sense of patience? When working with junior players, the teacher should emphasize the fun aspects of the game. Does the teacher let them hit balls with all of the clubs so they become comfortable with them? Most importantly, does the teacher let the child pick the part of the game that he/she wants to learn first?

Does the teacher get the child and parents involved in our games? This is the most powerful way for them to both bond and to keep the child interested.

Lesson R$_x$

Whatever form your instruction takes, you need a clear idea about the tips, suggestions, and skills to integrate into your swing. The better instructors and golfing schools will give written feedback and skill development ideas to follow after the lesson. These assignments should suggest drills, thoughts, games, or specific swing mechanics with guidance on how to acquire and retain them. This can include specific suggestions to carry with you to practice and then take to the course.

One way to do this is to write a prescription, like your doctor gives you. You should get a prescription after each lesson, maybe even several, depending on the nature of the lesson and what game elements were covered. Here is an example:

Final Thought

Our final comment about picking a golf coach: *you must be comfortable with the coach and see progress in your game.* If your game is not improving, it is time two ask two questions:

- Is the failure due to poor advice or lack of rapport? If "Yes," seek another teacher.
- Is the failure a result of poor execution of good advice? If "Yes," read Chapter 12 to learn how to practice more effectively.

12
Perfecting Your Practice

Comments by Ben Hogan[1] in a 1987 interview with Nick Seitz, reprinted in the October, 1997 Golf Digest:

Seitz: *There is a modern theory that when you warm up before a round you don't want to be worried about your swing; you just want to get loose. But it was serious practice with you, wasn't it?*

Hogan: *I didn't just go out there and hit balls. I tried to narrow this thing down. If I aimed to a tree out there, I wanted to try and hit that tree. Because that is what you do on the golf course: You aim at a specific target.*

Seitz: *You were thinking target with every practice ball?*

Hogan: *That's right, because you do it on the golf course. Why go out there and merely take calisthenics and run to the first tee?*

> ***Practicing**:* an activity in which you actively repeat some skill with the goal of either improving or maintaining it.

Reading this chapter will help you to:

- Grasp the basic elements of effective practice.
- Understand how to develop an efficient, effective practice routine.
- Integrate our games into your practice routine.

---

[1] Ben Hogan (1912–1997), American golfer, generally considered one of the greatest players in the history of the game, noted for his influence on the golf swing theory and legendary ball-striking ability.

Introduction: Effective Practice Technique

Many believe they can read about a golfing technique or see it on TV, and then duplicate it on the course. This is a mistake.

The only way to develop or maintain any skill is to practice it, and practice it efficiently. The goal of this chapter is to give you basic information on how you can develop your golf game through effective practice technique.

In our *Tech Talk,* we puncture the myth of the perfect swing. We conclude with recommendations for a successful practice strategy that you can personalize to developing, enhancing, and maintaining your game.

Tech Talk: The Perfect Swing

Iron Byron is a robot used by the United States Golf Association to test golf clubs and balls to make sure they conform to official standards. It can be adjusted to make thousands of repeatable golf swings. Unfortunately, none of us can compete with the reliability of a robot, but we all want it to be as consistent as possible. The harsh fact is: no one from *beginner* to touring pro has a perfectly repeatable shot. What distinguishes the better players from the less skilled ones is that their shots are less erratic.

These two pictures compare a player with an inconsistent swing to a player with a consistent one. Here we have illustrated two hypothetical players who hit ten balls with the same club to a target 20 yards away.

| Inconsistent player | Consistent player |

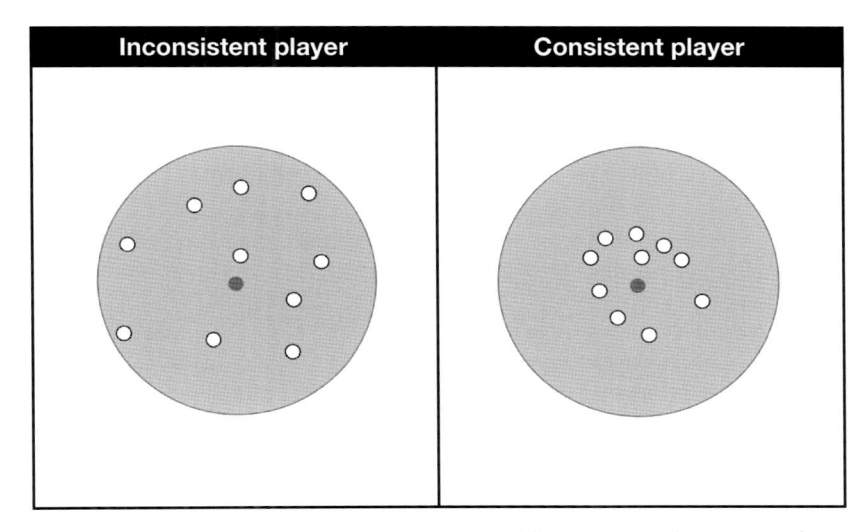

Since neither player has a perfect swing, the hits are spread out around the target. The inconsistent player's balls are more scattered around the target than are those of the consistent golfer. This highlights an important fact. **Consistency is a prerequisite to a good score, but does not guarantee it**. If you constantly hit a duck hook, you have achieved repeatability but your scores will be terrible. To develop a consistent swing you have to practice and practice well. As we will point out later many golfers do not know how to make the most effective use of their time on the range. Before we describe the efficient practice techniques we want to review what you should be practicing.

The Role of Aids, Tips, Drills, Practice, and Games

When you watch the Golf Channel or other televised golfing events, you cannot avoid commercials and infomercials that talk about some mechanical aid that is designed to help us swing more efficiently. These range from fuzzy tees, to hinged and weighted clubs, to straps and harnesses. Many of these can be useful for improving a swing. Yet, once we are practicing and playing, we still have to hit the ball on our own.

In addition to equipment, there are many programs and articles that give game improvement hints, tips, drills, and practice suggestions. There are so many suggestions that it is difficult to put them into context.

What is the difference between a tip, drill, and game?

Tips are brief swing improvement recommendations. Every golf magazine has a series of excellent brief suggestions on how to play better. There are books full of tips and swing hints. One book offers a collection of more than 400 swing ideas covering a host of golfing situations. The typical tip will tell you what to do but not how to do it. An example is advising players to use a fairway club to putt from off the green. This can be a good idea, but it does not tell you much about the mechanics of the stance, grip and the swing needed to successfully perform this shot. **Better golfing tips tell you what to do and how to do it, but they are not much help unless you fully develop them through practice.**

> When practicing, use the club that gives you the most trouble, not the one that gives you the most satisfaction.
>
> —Harry Vardon

Another level of golfing advice comes from drills. Most of us have spent time doing these brief exercises designed to perfect some basic element of the golf swing. They generally do not involve the full swing, only one piece of it. A recent Google search using the key phrase "golf drills" yielded a million and a half hits. They focused on a variety of topics: weight shift drills, power turn drills, swing tempo drills, slice correction drills. Drills can improve your game, but they do not reflect the full golf swing, only one element of it. **Preoccupation with drills can overwhelm the natural flow of an automatic swing**. Like good tips, to be effective drills must be integrated into the full golf swing.

One step up in complexity from the drill is full-swing practice. Countless golfers can be seen practicing on and around the green or hitting at a practice facility. The goal of these activities should be to enhance your swing by making it automatic. Disappointments sometimes come when we go from the range to the first tee. Somehow those wonderful arcing shots seem to have abandoned us. To be most effective, practice must be done in a situation that is as close to the game played on the course as possible. The key is **practice what you play and play what you have practiced.** This will enhance transfer to your game on the course and lower your score.

One of the reasons that our range expertise deserts us is that most of us spend too much time on our favorite shots and not enough time on those shots we need to perfect. These favorites are the ones we hit well; they reinforce us. We tend to avoid working with the problem clubs and shots because the frustration of swinging them poorly is discouraging. **To become a skilled golfer we need to practice with all of the clubs, not just the favorites**. Our intermediate and advanced games encourage you to use all of your clubs, not just the friendly ones.

> It is the constant and undying hope for improvement that makes golf so exquisitely worth playing.
>
> —Bernard Darwin

A second drawback is that traditional practice is a solitary activity. Playing golf is a social competition. For practice to match the playing environment, it should be social and should involve some level of friendly rivalry. Our games provide the competitive setting that you usually find on the course.

The most important reason that the swing we loved on the range does not travel to the course is that **on the range there are no consequences for mistakes**. The range gives us endless mulligans. On the course each shot has a consequence. Good shots help our score, bad shots hurt our score. The impact of a good or bad shot adds a level of pressure not found during the typical practice session. Our games, whether played competitively or alone, provide the pressure you would find on the course. This is because our games**,** like the Saturday round with friends, have standards of performance that you must meet to be successful.

Please understand, aids, drills, practice, and repetition are essential for gaining confidence and creating patterns that ensure an automatic golf swing. But, we also feel that there are other things you can do to develop your swing that go beyond practice, and these are our 101 Golf Games.

The Practice Process

Practicing golf is the process of repeating the swing elements you want to learn with the goal of making them automatic. There are two basic goals of practice.

The first is to develop and imbed the mechanics of a new golf swing. We call this **developmental practice**. It is the phase where you are trying to learn a new swing technique. It applies to both the beginning golfer who is acquiring basic swing skills and the accomplished player who is making fundamental swing changes.

The second goal of practice is to maintain a swing that has already been acquired and is well learned. This is called **maintenance practice**. There are slightly different approaches to practicing the new swing and the well-learned one, but the outcome of each is similar—making the swing so natural that the player doesn't have to think about it. This is *Automaticity*: making some action so routine that you can perform it without thought.

You can probably ride a bicycle without thought about steering, balance, braking, and pedaling. The skill is automatic, a far cry from the first time you sat on one and wobbled your way down the street while worried about the possibility of skinned knees and a bumped head. Unfortunately, most golfers do not know the best way to practice in a way to make their golf swings automatic. Here are three basic mistakes that people often make.

- In spring the golfer grabs his clubs out of the basement as soon as the weather gets above 40° and heads for the range. After several buckets of balls he feels he is ready for the season. While this effort may help to identify the muscles that have been hibernating, it does nothing to enhance the game. **This is fantasy practice**.
- A second approach is to take a new swing element, rehearse it intensely for an hour Friday evening, with the expectation that it will

show up on the course on Saturday morning. To our surprise, the swing has been lost overnight. **This is called *massed practice*;** all of the effort is done intensely over a brief period of time. **It is the equivalent to cramming for an exam**. The skill may be there temporarily but is soon lost.

Folks practicing this way are the ones most likely to wail, "I did this well yesterday, why can't I do it today?"

> Learn fast—forget quick.
> —Chinese proverb

There is, however, one benefit of massed practice. It leads to **rapid initial learning**. This is why a new golf skill should be rehearsed as soon as possible after it is taught. Yet, there is a major drawback of this approach; unless the practice is spaced over time, massed practice does not lead to permanent learning (retention). Relying on one-time, intense practice will inevitably lead to disappointment.

- A third flawed practice technique is to take a couple of clubs to the range once a month and hit a large bucket of balls assuming that this effort will groove the swing permanently. This is not practice, it is exercise.

For learners and people acquiring a major new golf swing, practice is no different than weight training in the gym. For muscle development the most successful approach is to take a target weight and bench press it a fixed number of times, rarely more than eight to twelve repetitions. Then the person moves on to another exercise rotating through the muscle groups, focusing relatively briefly on each group. Like the weight trainer, **the best form of practice to learn a swing is to break it into frequent brief sessions rather than one intense marathon**.

Working out across several limited exercises is called **distributed practice.** For people hoping to make a swing automatic, the best way is to hit each shot a limited number of times, move on to another club, and then return. Here is an example of how this can work.

Lynn wants to eliminate skulled chips. Lynn's instructor shows her how to execute the chip shot properly by showing her how to alter her swing: tweaking ball placement, weight distribution, swing, and follow through.

PERFECTING YOUR PRACTICE

There are two ways Lynn could practice this shot. The first would be to perform it intensely for 60 minutes (massed practice). Second, she could practice it separately six times for ten minutes with a break between each session (distributed practice). This break could be the shift to another club or a five-minute rest. The amount of time is the same, but **breaking the practice into separate brief sessions will lead to much more permanent acquisition and retention**. There are several reasons that this distributed approach is more effective.

> If profanity had an influence on the flight of the ball, the game would be played far better than it is.
>
> —Horace G. Hutchinson

- Lynn stays more alert. Anything we do repetitively over time is boring and we lose our focus. Revisiting that activity over several brief periods helps to maintain our concentration.
- Lynn is less likely to become fatigued. Her energy level will be as consistent as it would be on the course.
- Lynn has more opportunities to practice. Short time blocks are more likely to be available than hour-long time periods.

How to Practice for Improvement

In one on the most scientifically rigorous articles summarizing how to practice for improvement, K. Anders Ericsson wrote:

> From a review of studies of learning and skill acquisition, we found evidence for consistent gradual improvement of performance when the following conditions were met. First, the participants were instructed to improve some aspect of performance for a well-defined task. Second, they were able to get detailed immediate feedback on their performance. Finally, they had ample opportunities to improve their performance gradually by performing the same or similar tasks repeatedly. The participants were able to keep improving their performance during extended training as long as the training sessions were limited to around an hour.[1]

[1] *Deliberate Practice and the Acquisition and Maintenance of Expert Performance in Medicine and Related Domains,* Academic Medicine, VOL . 79 , NO. 10 /October Supplement 2004

The meaning of this research for golfers who want to improve is that effective practice has five elements:

1. You need expert instruction (Chapter 11).

2. You should practice new swing elements as soon as possible after a lesson. The old saying, *Use it or lose it*, certainly applies to the golf swing.

3. While practicing you should get immediate feedback. This is not hard to do with a golf shot. However, the best feedback comes from a competent coach who can give advice on how to correct any flaws either during or immediately after the practice session.

4. Repetition is important to developing an automatic shot. This is especially true for the expert golfer who wants to maintain a high performance level.

5. Practicing specific shots should be spaced over time—distributed practice.

If you go the driving range and hit a large bucket of balls with no systematic plan, you are wasting your time. The practice green and driving range are not there for you to get exercise. They are there for you to enhance your game by building swing confidence and consistency. This must be done just as systematically as the person in the gym's weight training room who focuses on specific muscle groups. Here is what we recommend.

1. Decide what **elements of your swing need work, the shots you want to improve, or the new shots you need to develop.** The best source of information for this is your teacher or coach. Your instructor should even suggest some of the games that will help you. You can also use the Swing Inventories in Chapter 9. You should plan to do this swing practice in three to six separate sets of ten to fifteen balls per set.

2. **Make a practice list** similar to the one we have shown below. It should identify the clubs you want to hit and your goal for hitting them. For example, "Hit my driver using the flat wrist adjustment to minimize

my slice" or "*Play the Putting in the Dark game making 8 to 15-yard putts concentrating on swinging with my shoulders, not my wrists, to gain better control.*" For people who are learning the basic elements of the swing, ask your teacher to give you a list of the swing elements to concentrate on. The *Swing Prescription Pad* is shown at the end of Chapter 11 is a good model for this assignment. Your teacher should also give you some hints to help you diagnose what causes mistakes. Now you will know what you are doing, why you are doing it, and the result you expect.

Here is an example of a practice list we recommended to Fran, an experienced player who was having difficulty hitting long fairway shots and had lost confidence in close-in short pitches.

1. **7-iron.** Hit to within seven yards of 145 yard marker using correct alignment.

2. **4 rescue club.** Hit to within 15 yards of 180 yard marker keeping full turn.

3. **Sand wedge.** Hit 30 yards to a 12-foot target using correct alignment.

4. **Pitching wedge.** Hit 50 yards to a 15-foot target focusing on alignment.

5. **Play *Pitching: Up and Down*** to earn 20 points from 10 yards.

3. **Warm up** by swinging a favorite club and then doing a couple of stretching exercises. Then hit a couple of balls with your favorite club starting with easy strokes until all of the kinks are worked out of your body and you feel loose.

4. **Work through your practice list**. Hit each shot ten to fifteen times and then move on to the next one. You should repeat the list at least three times per practice session. Keep track of your good shots as well as the poor ones. It is OK to make mistakes on the range. It is better to make them there than on the course! The key is to learn from them.

- **DO:** Take notes on what works. This might focus on body feel, position, swing thought, alignment or any of the elements of the swing that worked for you. This will help you recall the feeling of a successful shot.
- **DO:** Focus on the feeling your body experienced when you hit a good shot. This is the physical memory you want to take to the course.
- **DO:** Take notes on miss-hits and what happened. How did it feel different from the good shot? You should also record what you tried to do that did and did not work for you. This is the information you need to take to your coach or teacher. The best way to keep track of your progress is to use our *Practice and Performance Diary*. You can use it to record your practice sessions and performance on the course.

5. **Go back to some of your favorite clubs and hit them**. It is important to complete a practice round with a sense of confidence.
6. **Play one of our games.** Our games will set a standard of performance that will help you to feel more confident on the swing skills you are developing.

When Should I Practice?

We recommend that you practice as soon after a lesson as possible and plan to schedule follow-up practice sessions within a week or two. It is also good to take new swing ideas to the course. Think of this course play as a dress rehearsal or a trial run to try out your new swing. This will take some of the pressure off of believing that you must play flawlessly.

The ideal sequence would be *lesson–practice–on-the-course–practice.* This sequence will help you to both retain and transfer new golfing skills to the course.

One effective technique is to carry a card listing the key swing ideas you are focusing on and refer to it both on the range and on the course. If you want to build confidence in your swing, you need to commit to these ideas, and this card will help you keep them in mind.

How Will I Know If My Practice Is Paying Off?

Noted golf commentator David Feherty once said, *"Ever notice how people practice until they think they get it right? Why don't we practice until we don't do it wrong?"* If you follow our recommendations you should see positive results from your practice sessions pretty quickly. But, you are not successful if you hit a shot well only once. You should take Feherty's quote to heart and think about practicing until you see your mistakes becoming fewer and fewer. When Marilyn was learning how to hit greenside bunker shots she knew she was mastering them shot when the number of successful shots rose from every other shot, to three in a row to six, and eventually she could executed the shot consistently without error. It took time, but her progress was measured in the number of consecutive correct shots.

KEY LEARNING POINT!!!

If you consistently make the same mistake and don't know what's wrong, **STOP HITTING THAT SHOT!** Go to another form of practice.

Why? If you keep at it, you will replace a good swing with the mistake, and build frustration with that club. You should not be discouraged by these mistakes. This is the information you need to take to your teacher for a repair session.

Go to your instructor to identify the mistake you are making and how to fix it. Then integrate this fix into your next practice.

Practice for the Expert Player

For the *Skilled* and *Expert* player, practice takes on a slightly different focus. Accomplished players—including competitive golfers—should focus on maintaining their swing. If you are a skilled golfer, your primary goal is not to acquire golf skill. It is to *preserve and enhance your ability to predict and control golf shots.* Your practice goal is to **overlearn the swing** until it is so automatic that it can be done without thought.

A good maintenance technique is to develop a standard for each series of practice shots. One player we know uses this short game routine: He selects spots 10, 15, and 20 yards from the green and challenges himself to hit two balls up-and-in from each location. If he misses any shot, he starts over again. This is called **practicing to criterion.** The criterion is a standard that must be achieved before the practice round is over. In this example, the criterion is hitting up and down in no more than two strokes. Other examples are making ten 4-foot putts in a row from different locations, or driving twelve balls to a specific target area.

The benefit of practicing to criterion is that it includes the element of *practicing with consequence*. It brings in the element of pressure that you would find on the course and in competition.

Many of our games can be modified for criterion-related practice. Here are some that can be played alone or with a partner. The numbers in front of the game help you find them in the booklet.

Putting Booklet
- 1 Putting in the Dark
- 12 Speed Putting
- 16 Mishmash
- 17 Up-and-In

Chipping Booklet
- 7 In-the-Pits
- 9 Up-And-Down
- 14 Chipping Trifecta
- 17 Shank

Pitching Booklet
- 7 Swamp Monster
- 9 Pitch Off the Old Block
- 10 Up and In
- 19 Long Shot

Full Swing Booklet
- 5 Variety Pack
- 7 Rip It
- 10 Bulls Eye
- 12 Liar
- 15 Big Three

Bunker Booklet
- 5 Over the Dunes
- 8 Triple Play
- 14 Bunker Blast
- 15 Dealer's Choice

Our final comment is that **practice without a goal is, at best, a warm-up.** Whenever you go to a practice area you should have a clear idea of what you want to accomplish and how you intend to do it.

Getting Ready to Hit: The Pre-Shot Routine

Denise was a mid-90s golfer with a decent fundamental swing. When being interviewed at the beginning of her first golf lesson, her teacher, Betsy, asked Denise about the swing thoughts she had as part of her pre-shot routine.

After a moment's reflection, Denise said she usually mentally reviewed about 15 to 20 things before hitting the ball. When Betsy asked her about which ones were most important she replied, "All of them."

Over the next three lessons, Betsy helped Denise reduce the number of swing thoughts to three key ideas. As a result her ball striking became more consistent as she became more focused on the total swing and not its pieces.

Reading this chapter will help you to:

- Understand how thoughts, emotions, and swing mechanics all interact to influence your golf game.
- Recognize the need for a pre-shot routine.
- Develop your own personalized pre-shot routine.

Introduction: The Pre-Shot

Watch professional golfers as they get ready to hit the ball. If you time them, there is no more than a second or two difference between the time they address the ball until they swing at it. In a recent television interview one of the greatest women players, Annika Sorenstam, said that it takes her exactly 24 seconds from the time she takes a club out of the bag until she swings at the ball.

All of the mental planning and mechanical preparation we go through for each shot is part of our pre-shot routine. While there are almost as many pre-shot routines as there are golfers, there is one constant. Every golfer has one.

The pre-shot routine is everything you do to get ready to hit the golf ball. It begins well before you address the ball or even stand behind it. It starts as soon as you decide to step on the first tee. It begins again as soon as you hit a drive and see where the ball lands and get ready to make the next stroke. Having a repeatable shot is great, but choosing when to use this shot is part of the pre-shot routine.

As we pointed out in Chapter 10, planning and goal setting are an important part of learning, developing, and practicing your golf game. Effective practice technique is another requirement. Yet, knowing how to hit a ball consistently is only one facet of playing well. Another key element of scoring low is developing an effective pre-shot routine.

Why Is the Pre-Shot Routine Important?

The pre-shot routine is important for several reasons.

1. It forces you to focus on the current shot and clear your mind of outside distractions. Anything that diverts your attention from the swing will harm the shot.

2. It forces you to concentrate on the key elements of the shot: your lie, the wind, course conditions, the club you should use, your target, the feel of the swing, your set-up and alignment.

3. It provides a consistent beginning to a repeatable stroke. All golfers want a consistent swing. This consistency must begin with the prelude to making the shot. The prelude is the pre-shot routine.

The pre-shot routine has two basic components.

First, "Where do I want the ball to be after I swing at it?" With putting, the answer here is pretty basic: put the ball into the hole. For other shots, the answer may be more complicated, focusing on decisions such as I need to be on the right side of the fairway to avoid the bunker over there. Or, "I need to chip this ball three feet onto the green to roll it close to the hole." These decisions are course strategy and game management decisions, the first elements of the pre-shot routine.

The second element of the pre-shot routine is, "How do I get the ball there?" The answer depends a huge number of factors including your skill level, the ball's position, course conditions, the clubs you have confidence in, and your target area.

Developing Your Pre-Shot Routine

An effective pre-shot routine has five characteristics. We call this **SCRAP:** Simple, Consistent, Realistic, Automatic, and Personal:

Simple: As we have pointed out, too much thinking gets in the way of an effective stroke. Too much analysis will hinder your commitment to a shot. Generally newer players have a multitude of ideas and thoughts they review as they prepare to hit the ball. This is a result of not having an automatic swing. More experienced players have confidence in their swings. As a consequence, they can limit themselves to only a few key ideas to help them focus on the shot, not swing mechanics. Their pre-shot thoughts are much more focused. Trying to consciously review everything you have learned about the stroke will overload your brain.

Consistent: Most players want to have a repeatable swing, but they don't understand that the way they prepare for the swing influences its consistency. **You should mentally prepare yourself for each shot the same way every time**. If you have a consistent pre-shot routine it becomes a part of the swing itself. As you should know by now, consistency leads automatic swings, and automatic swings give successful shots and lower scores.

Realistic: **You should play within your game.** Decide what shot you have to make and select your most well-learned shot rather than one you *might* make. Realism leads to confidence and confidence is essential for commitment to the shot.

Automatic: You should not have to think about your routine. You should consider the same elements the same way every time. This means you should **integrate it into your practice on the range and do not drag it out of your bag at the last moment on the course**.

Personal: Just as no one swing fits all people, **no single routine fits all people**. While every pre-shot routine will include, "Where do I want to be?"

and "How do I get there?" the rest is up to you. The routine can be very precise, organized, meticulous, and methodical or it can be very quick if that is your preference. It should mirror your personality and playing style.

Tech Talk: Psychology of the Pre-Shot Routine

Before we get into a discussion of the pre-shot routine we need to explain three basic elements of physical performance: thoughts, emotions, and swing mechanics. All three are interconnected and influence each other to either enhance your game or bring it to its knees.

Thoughts

Thoughts are the logical, and occasionally illogical, ideas and beliefs we have. They are an inevitable part of the pre-shot routine. There are many things we think about when playing golf. They can include worries about a job, chats with a playing partner, or what we would like to do for the next holiday. When we start thinking about how to hit the ball we have moved to swing thoughts. **Swing thoughts are all of the plans, ideas, and beliefs we have about the next shot**.

> I never really dreamed of making many putts. Maybe that's why I haven't made many."
>
> —Calvin Peete

One category of swing thoughts consists of the technical tips that focus on the mechanical parts of the game: "Remember to take a full turn," or ,"Keep my weight on my left side," or, "Slow down my backswing." For developing players it is OK to have multiple thoughts when practicing, especially technical tips. This is where you are learning your swing - integrating the elements so they become an automatic part of your swing. On the other hand, having too many swing thoughts when you are trying to hit the ball during a game can lead to confusion. Try to limit them on the course so they do not become a distraction and interfere with total commitment to the stroke.

A second group of swing thoughts deals with course management: "I've got to hit to the right to stay clear of that bunker." "How should I play this break?" "Should I lay up or go for the green?" "Which way is the wind blowing and how should I adjust for it?" These are the decisions we make for each shot. They are influenced by our skill, knowledge, and experience. This is the true thinking part of the game. Failures here usually result in the murmur, "What was I thinking?"

Unfortunately, **too much thinking gets in the way of an automatic strike at the ball**. The more you practice, the more automatic the swing becomes and the less you need to rely on multiple mental reminders about how to hit the ball effectively. This is the automaticity we talked about in Chapter 12.

Emotions

Emotions are the feeling part of our lives. They include such things as love, anger, worry, joy, and desire. They focus on parts of the game that are not mechanical. Positive emotions can enhance your game. Being optimistic about a shot over a ravine breeds confidence and will encourage a successful shot. Many thoughts are helpful in establishing positive emotions. For example, saying to yourself, "I know I can hit the green with this iron, I have done it hundreds of times," or, "This five foot putt is a piece of cake because I have made it 1,000 times in practice." lead to calm, positive feelings and reduce tension. Good swing thoughts help you build your confidence by generating an encouraging mood. These thoughts are not only useful, they are necessary both on the practice range and the course.

Negative emotions are game killers. They can start with pessimistic thinking that leads to gloom:

"I must hit this shot well to win the hole" encourages anxiety.

"I hope I am not slowing up the group" encourages worry.

"These people are much better than I am; I look like a deranged octopus playing with a popsicle stick compared to them" will be demoralizing.

"I am really doing well now, but something is bound to go wrong" is a self-fulfilling prophecy.

Things will go wrong if you believe they will. Golfers can dwell on downbeat ideas every day or even weeks before an event. We do a more thorough analysis of negative emotions in Chapter 14.

Some players, especially in highly competitive rounds, use mental diversions to help keep them calm. Some will think of calm cool places, others will keep songs in their minds, while still others daydream about things other than golf. These mental diversions help to keep the dark, emotional thoughts at bay. Other players use motivational ideas. These are inspirational beliefs such as, "Believe in yourself!" and "This is my bread-and-butter shot; I know I can make this one!" These help a player focus on success and lead to emotional commitment.

Sometimes these diversions take the form of superstitions. Dennis does not use a tee that another player has left in the ground on the tee box; he won't even reset it. Jan always wipes the head of her irons twice with a towel, no matter how shiny they are. If these odd behaviors help you relax and focus, then use them; they can't hurt your game.

Swing Mechanics

As we said in Chapter 11, swing mechanics are the motor skills involved in the physical act of hitting that little white ball. We learn swing mechanics from teachers, coaches, and other players and perfect those mechanics through drills, practice, games, and playing on the course. The more we practice, the more automatic our swing becomes and the less we have to think about how to perform it.

Putting it Together

The three performance elements—thoughts, emotions, swing mechanics—are independent of each other. Yet they interact to influence our play and

Performance Circle
Thoughts ↔ Emotions
Swing Mechanics

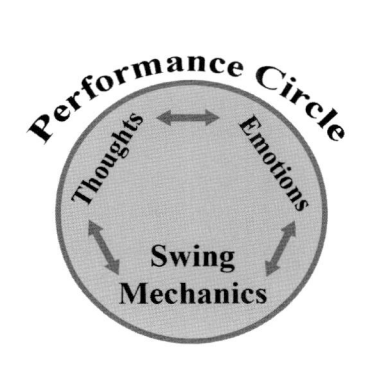

everything we do.

Think about a time you played a front nine and were shooting your best score ever. Your thoughts about swing mechanics were probably close to zero; the swing just happened almost effortlessly. You were probably thinking pretty positively about yourself (emotions). Then, starting on the tenth hole, your putter turned into a piece of overcooked linguini and started doing strange things!

Your great round was interrupted by three putts. You started getting upset (emotions), so you started reviewing how you were addressing the ball and your putting stroke (thoughts). The more you thought the less consistent your swing became (mechanics) which led to more indecision, more thinking, and more frustration all of which led to more erratic putts.

A major reason for this entire game change is that our brains have a limited space for processing information. While we can store a huge amount data, we can process only a limited amount of it at one time. The three performance elements each take up a portion of this area.

This is the reason why our swing gets poorer when we hold more thoughts about it. **We have a limited amount of processing area to do all of this mental, emotional, and physical work. If one element begins to dominate, it comes at the expense of the others**.

Pre-Shot Routine Sequence

Whenever you start thinking about your next shot, you are in some phase of the pre-shot routine. Whether you are consciously aware of it or not your pre-shot routine has all three performance elements: thoughts, emotions, and mechanics. Their relationship and the importance of these elements change as you get closer to hitting the ball. To help you understand this we have broken the routine into four separate phases: Approach, Commitment, Address, and Swing.

Approach

In this phase you are either walking to a tee or have just hit a ball and are getting ready for your next shot.

Thinking—Swing thoughts usually predominate here. As you approach the tee, or the place where the ball has landed, you start analyzing the lie and try to determine what your next shot will be. Your thoughts focus on the club to use, shot to make, influence of the lie, and where the shot must land.

Emotions—You may feel good or bad about the shot and the lie. Unless you have completely blown it, you will have some positive thoughts or perhaps some element of worry if the lie is not great. If the shot has been terrible, you may feel the sense of frustration or anger with yourself, the fickle club, or the errant ball.

Mechanics—Mechanics generally don't play a major role here. You probably have not decided on a specific shot or club so any level of physical rehearsal is not a factor yet.

Commitment

When you get to the ball, the relationship between all three elements change.

Thinking—Swing thoughts are important now. You have to decide what club to use, what kind of stroke you want to make, and a target to hit for. For putting, you have to decide on the line and speed of the stroke. You may consider the influence of the wind, course conditions, ball lie etc. You may mentally rehearse some swings, visualize the shot, or review some key swing mechanics. At this point you decide on a particular shot using a particular club and a particular target location. This is called **total commitment to the shot**. If you are not committed you will find yourself mulling over multiple shot possibilities. This creates indecision. When combined with preoccupation with multiple swing ideas, indecision will inevitably lead to a poor shot.

Emotions—The emotional level may or may not change. If you are in the ideal zone where you are focused on the game and are feeling confident, then your emotions will help you focus. On the other hand, if you are playing double or nothing on a hole and have a 165-yard shot to a tiny green surrounded by sand bunkers five feet deep and need to make a great shot, the pressure may be intense. This may create muscle tension that can get in the way of your swing. **Positive emotional commitment to the shot you know you can make will reduce doubt and the pressure**.

Mechanics—Your goal here is to capture the feel of the shot you plan to make. You may take out a club and swing it a couple of times to get a feel for the shot and then make a decision about the stroke you will make. We call this the **commitment to the swing.** You physically rehearse either all or elements of the shot you have in mind and decide, "This is how I will hit the ball."

If the swing feels right, your commitment increases. If the practice swing feels wrong, then you will question yourself and these thoughts will divert your attention. The indecision can create tension; the birth of a bad shot. The key solution here is to back off and start the Commitment phase again.

Address

Address is the position you take when you stand over the ball preparing to hit it. You have selected a club and should be committed to a shot. Your focus is on hitting the ball to your target area.

Thinking—You are fully committed to the shot and swing. You may have one or two swing thoughts. You may briefly check your alignment, recall a specific feel, or reconfirm the target area.

Emotions—You have positive, confident feelings.

Mechanics—You may have one or two reminders for the mechanics of the shot you have chosen. Some players make a slight rehearsal to remind them of the feel they want. Others "waggle" the club as a reminder to relax.

Generally, the time you take at *Address* should be brief. Of course, if your ball is surrounded by rabid squids and it will cost you a penalty stroke to move it, then your time at address may take a bit longer. Standing over the ball at *address* for too much time will lead to overthinking, tension, and/or indecision. If this happens, back off and start the *commitment* phase again.

Swing

This is the stroke. It calls for intense focus and eliminating all but one or two thoughts.

Thinking—You have one or two final thoughts before the swing starts. Some people have a mental or physical trigger they use to initiate the backswing and/or downswing. This may be a slight forward press which acts as a brief physical reminder for one or two swing cues or a reminder such as "slow back" or "hip turn to start shot". These vary from individual to individual.

Emotions—At this point you should be emotionally calm. The feelings of success should be at the forefront of your thoughts.

> After taking the stance it is too late to worry. The only thing to do then is hit the ball.
>
> —Bobby Jones

Mechanics—The automatic, unconscious mechanics of the swing take over and dominate as you swing. **For the player who has prepared well through instruction and practice, this is where physical automaticity takes over.** There is no hesitation and the shot is truly thoughtless.

At this point, if you have the slightest doubt or hesitation then you should step away from the ball and begin your routine again to regain *Commitment* to the shot.

The time between address and swinging at the ball should be no more than four to eight seconds. If it takes longer, then you probably have some doubts and you should back away and start over again. Whatever the time, you should be consistent. Hurrying the stroke will lead to mis-hits; spending too much time will generally lead to second guessing, over thinking and/or lack of commitment.

This analysis highlights one important thing. **Hitting the ball without total**

mental, emotional, and mechanical commitment usually results in a poor shot. Standing over the ball at address and rethinking the shot will have an impact on your confidence and commitment. Second guessing will interfere with an automatic, natural stroke.

You will frequently see experienced players stand at address then back away from the ball. They have started commitment process again. The essential characteristic commitment is total concentration on the selected shot with no outside thoughts or doubts. This is why many golfers insist on quiet. Noises, conversation, shouts, gusts of wind can all interrupt this focus. If this happens, the best response is to back away to reset your concentration.

The Role of Physical Rehearsal

We could not finish this section without commenting on the important role that physical rehearsal plays in a pre-shot routine. **Rehearsal is swinging the club with the goal of recapturing the feel of the shot without actually hitting the ball.** The rehearsal may include either the full swing or elements of it. You should integrate physical rehearsal into your pre-shot routine and practice it both on and off the course. Effective rehearsal has the following elements.

- You have practiced it until it becomes automatic.
- You use it to capture the feel of one or two key elements of the swing.
- You integrate it into the *commitment* phase of your pre-shot routine. The closer the rehearsal is to the actual shot, the more effective it will be.

If the rehearsal feels wrong, you step back and identify the element that does not feel right. This uncomfortable feeling is your unconscious mind telling you that something is wrong. Begin the *commitment* phase again swing until you recapture the feel you are looking for. Typically this happens with the short game because these shots have more impact on you score.

Make as many rehearsals as you need to become confident with the swing. This is essential to developing total commitment to the shot. The number and format of rehearsal swings should be consistent. For example, Dennis always takes three practice swings while looking at the hole before putting, never four, never two. He uses these swings to remind him of the correct shoulder movement and alignment as well as to get a sense of the correct speed for the putt.

In closing, we want to remind you that all elements of your pre-shot routine should be directed toward success. Instead of thinking, "Don't dip my shoulder or I will hit the ball fat," say to yourself, "Rotate my shoulders for a solid shot." Instead of thinking, "I can probably hit the green if I really nail my 8-iron," shift to "I know I can make this shot with a 7-iron." We give you more ideas on positive thinking in the next chapter.

14
The Mental Game: Mind Over Swing

Mike, an avid weekend golfer, played with the Fearsome Foursome every Saturday. One beautiful day, he shanked a line drive into the middle of the club championship tennis match, almost hitting one of the players. The match paused while a ball boy retrieved the errant ball. After re-teeing a second ball, Mike took a mighty swing, hitting well under the ball, sending a high, arcing rainbow slice into the middle of the match—which had to be delayed again.

His playing partner, an insurance broker, laughed. "I will give you $100 if you can do that again!" To which Mike replied, "I'll give you $100 if you say it was you who hit the shot!" The humor defused Mike's tension, and he hit a decent shot into the middle of the fairway.

Reading this chapter will help you to:

- Identify and control unproductive swing thoughts.
- Understand the causes of stress and recognize the impact it has on your golf game.
- Name the different types of golf stressors and learn how to control them.
- Notice what causes frustration and recognize its impact on your game.

Managing Our Emotions

Arnold Palmer said it best: "Golf is a game of inches. The most important are those between the ears." In Chapter 13, we introduced the idea that cognitions (thinking and planning) and emotions are inevitable elements of your swing (even though they are occasionally hidden). In this chapter, we focus on the common negative thoughts and emotions we golfers experience, and suggest ways to deal with them.

Professional golfers get help with the emotional part of their games from a flock of advisors, coaches, and sports psychologists. The rest of us have to deal with the *mental game* on our own. We will help you understand, identify, and deal with thinking that can either help or harm your score:

- First, a summary of common positive and negative thoughts, and some ways to deal with them.
- Next, we have some Tech Talk on why it is so difficult to manage our emotions.
- Then we look at typical golfing stressors.
- Finally, we examine golfing frustration and its relationship to anger on the course.

Positive vs. Negative Thinking

As we said in Chapter 13, too many swing thoughts can be a problem. Positive, confident thoughts lead to a positive, confident approach to the game. But destructive thoughts create indecision, second-guessing, tension, negativity — and poor performance.

Here are examples of five common, harmful thoughts that frequently hound us. In each example, we have paired the negative thought with an alternative that helps you focus with confidence.

1. Dwelling on a Bad Shot Vs. Focusing on the Next Shot

If you spend time fretting over your last disappointing shot, then you might as well walk the course backwards, looking at where you have been, not where you are going. That is exactly how badly "dwelling on a bad shot" can hurt your game!

Instead, say to yourself that you are turning your back on it—it is gone. Walk away from that it and toward your next one!

> Golf is like a love affair. If you don't take it seriously, it's no fun; if you do take it seriously, it breaks your heart.
>
> —Arthur Daley

Another way to let go of "bad shot thinking" is to write it down and plan to review it later. (Try our simple record-keeping method in Chapter 9.)

When you finish a hole and are disappointed with your score, focus on the shots that went well, not the poor ones. One player we know uses this technique:

When he plays several bad holes in a row, he renumbers them on the scorecard and places a 1 for the next hole he plays. Then he tells himself, "OK, that round is over. Now I am starting a new game."

Another accomplished player we know stays focused by telling himself, "I know I am not playing well now, but I am a better player than this! I know this game. I'll turn it around."

2. "I'll get in trouble if I hit the ball over there" vs. "I'll be fine if I hit the ball to my target."

When you focus on possible problems, you overlook success. Keep your mind on where you want the ball to go, and avoid thoughts about where it might or shouldn't go. This is essential to good playing strategy and course management. If your practice has been to targets, then your play should be to targets.

3. "I can't hit this shot!" vs. "How can I make this shot?"

Focusing on what you *can't* do—we call it "can't thinking"—is futile. You can't fly, so don't waste time fretting about it. The same is true for a golf shot.

If your situation prevents you from hitting the ball where you want to hit it, then play it in a way you *can* hit it. Sometimes this takes creativity and imagination, but stop being negative and do what *can* be done.

Unless the ball is in an unplayable lie or in the mouth of a hippopotamus, "I can't" thinking comes from the mistaken belief that there is only one way to hit the ball in any situation. Not true!

For example, it might seem crazy to use a putter off the tee on a par five hole, but it *can* be done. Learning to think outside the box can give your game much more freedom.

In this book, many of our games encourage you to use several clubs for the same shot. For example, the following games give you opportunities to test yourself with a variety of clubs and trouble shots to broaden your shot-making confidence:

- *Chipping Trifecta* (*Chipping Booklet*)
- *Big Three* (*Full Swing Booklet*)
- *Bunker Triple Play* (*Bunker Booklet*)
- and several of our on-course games in the *On the Course Booklet*.

Try them!

Also, thinking "I might" is a close companion to "I can't." Saying "I might" shows lack of confidence, and for the thousandth time, confidence is essential for a successful golf shot. *Beginning* and *occasional* players often say "I might." This is understandable since they are still learning the fundamentals of a successful swing and may feel awkward when standing over the ball.

But stepping up to the ball and consciously saying, "*I will make the best swing I can*" removes the negativity of "*I might*." Hit the shot with the free swing feeling you worked on with your teacher and at the practice tee.

Another solution to these thought traps is to develop go-to shots**.** These are patterns that you can rely on, in even a cloudburst of frogs. Having an inventory of favorite, reliable shots increases your confidence when dealing with demanding situations, giving you a shot that falls in your comfort zone.

4. "I can't make mistakes" vs. "Mistakes are allowed."

"I can't make mistakes" is perfectionist thinking. Unless you are a calibrated robot like Iron Byron that can hit the same shot the same way 100% of the time, you are bound to make errant shots. This is especially true for *beginning* and *occasional* players. Change your thinking and live with it: mistakes are allowed!

In Chapter 12, we showed that superior and inferior shots can be expected from players at all levels. To quote the great golfing coach Harvey Penick, "If you play poorly one day, forget it. If you play poorly the next time—review your fundamentals of grip, stance, aim, and ball position. Most mistakes are made before the club is swung. If you play poorly for a third time—go see your professional."

Tell yourself, "I am not afraid to play poorly—but I am committed to playing well."

5. "I stink today; I can't play this game well" vs. "I am playing my best for me at the moment."

As you set foot on the first tee, think that you are going to play your best game for today and not the game you wish you had.

There are days when the golf gods bestow their blessings on other players, not you. Understand this and be content with what you have right now. You are playing your best at this moment. Your problems are not permanent. Be prepared for setbacks. Remember, *golf is a game of patience and persistence.*

You never know when your best game will become a reality. It might begin with the next stroke, or on the next hole. When you are playing poorly, always expect your next shot to turn your game around. When you feel that your swing has forsaken you, it's better to think, "I haven't played my best yet" than to think, "I can't play well at all."

Tech Talk: Where Your Negative Emotions Come From

Embarrassment, stress, and frustration are unwelcome acquaintances for every golfer; they are not our friends. Usually these emotions are fleeting companions, but they can cling like Velcro—persistent, unwelcome guests. Here's a brief Tech Talk on why these emotional interlopers are different from rational thoughts.

Your emotional life is mostly controlled in a primitive area deep in your brain called the limbic system. It controls your basic emotions—anger, fear, love, desire. This system is indirectly connected to the cerebral cortex, where your rational thinking (cognition) takes place. Neither system directly controls the other—which is why you cannot just think your worries away.

> The mind messes up more swings than the body.
> —Tommy Bolt

Think about that last sentence: The thinking part of your brain cannot override the emotional part. This is why you cannot take well-meaning advice like "Stop worrying about that shot—relax!" The thinking part of your brain may agree, but it cannot halt the niggling anxiety that makes you tense.

Problems arise when your negative emotions get out of control:

- They affect your ability to play well, creating body tension and reducing your game focus.
- They make you look foolish and embarrass you.
- They can distract other players.
- These emotional complaints and/or assaults on equipment are poor sportsmanship and lousy golf etiquette.
- They can destroy a game and even relationships faster than a shank.

Paradoxically, emotional arousal is your brain's way of protecting you! The primitive part of your brain does not distinguish between a hungry tiger, a tailgating car, or a five-foot putt to win a championship. The ancient part of your brain sees all of these as threats, and prepares you to deal with harm.

So your brain energizes your body to protect you. It's the famous *fight-or-flight* reaction.

Think about a time when someone has hit into you or your group without warning. You know that feeling of instant annoyance or anger. The primitive area of your mind leaps into action: "Danger! Threat!" and prepares you to fight or escape.

This uncontrollable reaction is immediate as your brain mobilizes your body to defend itself. Real or potential threats set off an involuntary chain of physiological changes: increased heart rate, blood flow diverted to your major muscles, and more sensitive vision. After the threat is gone, your body can take up to 20 minutes to "stand down" and relax.

The same thing happens when you lose your cool on the golf course. It will likely take you a hole and a half or more to calm down.

What does this mean for your game? In golf, when you are either too relaxed or too tense, you'll be off your game. Of the two, tension is worse, for even the smallest things can set you off.

Your ideal relaxation/tension level is somewhere between totally relaxed and aggressively tense. This ideal state varies from person to person.

It is difficult to manage this, and you can't do it by just reading about it. If that were possible, anyone could read *The Hogan Way* by John Andrisani and start swinging like Ben Hogan.

The way to learn emotional control is to get expert advice from a sports psychologist, practice that advice, and integrate it into your game.

Practicing emotional control on the golf course is as important to developing your game as practicing difficult flop shots.

Embarrassment

Embarrassment is a short-term emotional response. There are two elements of embarrassment. First, you made a mistake or did something you shouldn't have, and second, that someone saw you. Frequently this leads to a loss of dignity.

Embarrassment is that short-term feeling you get when your high arcing slice lands amidst a group of golfers in an adjacent fairway. Oops.

So you apologize and the group accepts it as you retrieve your ball. Then, either of two things happens. You have a clear shot to the green and your game has not been destroyed and the embarrassment melts away quickly, especially if your next shot is a winner. Or, you have a lousy shot and the humiliation just grows.

Regardless, here are three good techniques for dealing with embarrassment—laugh, joke, or do a reality check (maybe all three):

1. **Laugh**—Laughter is the easiest way to deal with embarrassing situations. Most of us laugh spontaneously anyway when we are embarrassed. Being able to laugh at yourself is the quickest way to recover.

   For example, Will was playing with eight friends. Will was getting ready to tee off on the tenth tee of a 370-yard par-four hole. The hole that had a pond 30 yards long in front of the tee box. Play had been slow that day, so there were three other groups waiting to tee off. Will's friends had teased him about weak drives for the past five holes. Taking out his trusty 3-wood, he took a mighty swing—topping the ball. It hit smack in the middle of the pond, skipped like a flat stone three times, jumped out of the pond, and rolled 30 yards down the fairway.

   His friends immediately doubled over with laughter. Will turned sheepishly and said, "That, ladies and gentlemen, is how you drive and clean your ball at the same time."

2. **Talk or joke**—Talk or joke about the situation briefly. Don't overdo it, but mentioning the situation to playing partners is one quick way to relieve your tension.

3. ***Do a reality check***—Most beginning golfers carry embarrassment like an extra club in their bags. This is especially true when they are with more experienced players. They forget that the better players were beginners at one time too, and that they tend to be tolerant and sympathetic toward the novice.

   It's a good thing to play with better golfers because you will learn from them. The key is to select partners who will be patient. These are the people who will be understanding, not judgmental.

Stress

Stress tends to outlast embarrassment and takes more effort to overcome.

Stress is your reaction to any demand or challenge that requires some sort of response. The demand can be external (your partner urges, "C'mon, hustle, we're holding up the group behind us!") or internal (you think, "I HAVE to sink this putt!").

There are two elements to stress:

- **Stressor**—you feel pressure to do something.
- **Response**—you believe you must react somehow to the stressor.

The emotional impact of stress varies from person to person. For example, giving a public speech causes huge stress in some while others feel no discomfort and enjoy the challenge.

Stress is not always bad. In fact, modest stress enhances your performance. Recall your stress response to a major exam back in school days. When the exam was a month away, you felt no pressure (stress) to study. But as the date approached, so did the pressure. If you began studying a day or two in advance, you felt modest pressure, but could focus on the material. However, if you began studying the hour before (e.g., cramming), your stress was much greater, and you probably found that you couldn't focus well, and your performance tanked.

So we have a clear relationship between your stress level and your performance. At one extreme, zero stress produces zero performance.

As the challenge to do something increases, so does the quality of your performance.

At some point, however, the stress becomes too great and your performance falls. This is what "stressed out" means. You feel that you can't deal with the pressure. When you hear the comment, "He choked," this is what is happening.

Stress and Your Game

So how does stress affect your golf game? Stress depends on two things: *your skill and the challenge.*

Both are highly individual—skill and challenge are all in how you perceive them:

Skill Level— *What you believe your ability level to be.* Some people hit a shot successfully twice and feel they have mastered it. Others need to hit it a thousand times to attain the same sense of skill.

Challenge— *How difficult you believe the shot to be.* For some, a flop shot over a greenside bunker is a piece of cake, while others see it as impossible. Challenge also relates to your playing environment. Playing for fun with friends can be a lot less challenging than playing for a championship.

For example, if your skill level is low and there is no challenge, you may feel no stress at all—you may be indifferent, relaxed, unconcerned. Say you are a *beginner* facing a one-inch tap-in putt on the practice green. The challenge and skill level required for this shot are both so low that you feel no stress, because the consequences of either success or failure are minimal.

But a *beginner* attempting a 50-yard approach shot to the green over a bunker will likely see it as difficult. The challenge is not too high, but as a *beginner's* skill is low and will feel the stress and grow tense.

In the same situation, the *expert* player will be relaxed and confident. This player recognizes the modest challenge, but his high skill level makes him comfortable with the shot. This low-stress situation leads to a relaxed mind and assured swing.

A Major Stress-Builder on the Course: "Must-Thinking"

There is a common form of thinking on the course that guarantees stress. We call it must-thinking. **MUST-THINKING refers to things you feel you absolutely have to do.**

There are tons of examples:

- "I MUST use a sand wedge out of a greenside bunker."
- "I MUST play as well as the rest of my group."
- "I MUST get par on this hole."

This kind of thinking is rigid, unforgiving—it leaves no room for error or compromise. The consequences to you are obvious: stress and extra pressure on your game. It may push you beyond your comfort zone. This usually leads to poor shots and frustration.

So, exactly why *must* you get par? Will the world be devoured by Godzilla if you don't? Are you playing to ransom the lives of your family from crazed aliens?

The easiest way out of *must-thinking* is to recognize it, to realize when it occurs. This is a major step in understanding that much of your stress is self-imposed.

Trying to make a difficult shot when that is your only alternative is understandable. But feeling that you MUST make that difficult shot when there is a safer alternative is usually self-defeating. Knowing and playing within your skill level leads to less stress and a more satisfying round of golf.

The substitute for must-thinking is can-thinking. Instead of thinking, "I MUST use my sand wedge to get out of this greenside bunker," try

THE MENTAL GAME: MIND OVER SWING

thinking, "How CAN I get out of this greenside bunker?" This makes your options blossom. You could use the sand wedge, but you might also use a putter or a seven-iron.

Can-thinking removes the pressure of focusing on only one option and lets you choose the most comfortable alternative.

Does this get you thinking differently? It should.

Coping with Stress

There are two fundamental coping strategies for stress: change the situation or change yourself. (Or, of course, do both.)

> Forget about your opponents. Always play against par.
> —Sam Snead

1. **Change the Situation.** Every time you hit a mulligan (replay a bad stroke), you are changing the situation by modifying golf rules to help you cope with a bad shot and enjoy playing. We have a friend who plays golf for the pure enjoyment of being outside and the companionship. He never writes down a score of more than twice par, takes frequent mulligans, and often adjusts the lie of the ball. *So, he changes the situation to enjoy the game.*

   Of course, changing the situation does not just mean ignoring or eliminating golf rules! Serious golfers and those working to establish a true handicap have legitimate ways to change the situation that fall within the standard rules of golf. These include changing clubs, balls, setup, game plan, playing partners, or courses.

2. **Change Yourself.** The second way to cope is to change yourself by developing your game. You can do this by taking lessons from a qualified teaching professional, playing our games, and/or practicing more effectively.

   Knowing what causes you stress on the course is the first step in dealing with it. Each of us has different golfing stressors, and we each have different ways of coping with them. For some golfers, a crowd of strangers watching on the first tee makes their chests tingle and hands go numb. For others, the crowd is motivating, energizing. Some folks play their best in competition, while others wilt under competitive pressure.

So the first step in dealing with your stressors is to identify them. Once identified, you can change the situation, or change yourself.

So What Are Your Golf Stressors?

We've broken stressors into four categories with some good ideas for coping with each: **Stressful Golfing Companions, Stressful Holes, Stressful Shots, and Stressful Environments.**

Stressful Golfing Companions

These are fellow golfers who cause you discomfort. Playing with them creates stress that interferes with your game. They can be players who give unnecessary advice, make irritating comments, complain constantly, or who golf at the speed of a constipated glacier.

> Sometimes you'd like to just stand there in the middle of the green and scream as loud as you can. But we're the perfect gentlemen.
> —Raymond Floyd

So let's apply our coping strategies: *change the situation or change yourself.* If you want to change the situation try to politely pointing out the other golfer's behavior, and ask them to stop. If you are among friends, you could initiate a friendly heart-to-heart with the other golfer to share your feelings.

Example 1: Roy played with Bob several times a year. Bob was likable and funny. But, whenever someone hit a putt short, Bob always muttered, *"You've got to HIT it, Alice!"* He found this very annoying—especially after the fourth time. Finally, Roy said, *"Bob, you've said that for the past three holes. I think I got the message."* So did Bob.

Example 2: Lou's golfing buddy loved to chat. However, this slowed play because he would conduct lengthy conversations before hitting the ball. Lou's frustration grew until one day he said, "Frank, the ranger is going to shoot you if you don't hurry up and hit the ball! We can finish your story after you hit."

Another option is to ignore the person's behavior. This is especially true when a playing partner consistently makes basic swing mistakes. You want to fix it, but know that the best advice is *requested* advice, not *offered* advice. So you keep quiet, mentally biting your tongue.

Learning how to be accepting of others' quirks and idiosyncrasies will help you to relax so that their flailings do not become contagious.

At worst, you can simply stop playing with your irritating companion.

So Hit the Damn Ball, Will Yuh? Another situation is the excessively deliberate player whose pre-shot routine takes longer than an elephant's courtship. John told one such golfer, "You know, if you take any longer to hit that ball, it is going to grow moss." Gently or directly talking to people whose behavior slows play sometimes works.

The Rule-Bound and the Rule-Free. Golfers who have "rule issues" can cause you stress—those who are either bound up in golfing rules, or who ignore them.

The Creeping Ball Marker

Joe played with a score-obsessed man, Bunker, who would flip his ball marker about 4–6 inches ahead of the ball when marking it on the green. After four such incidents, Joe said, "Bunk, if you keep marking the ball that way, your marker will end up in the cup. Why not keep it behind the ball?"

At one extreme you have the rules-obsessed golfer who knows all of the rules and comments on them regularly, often irritatingly, like the back-seat driver who reminds you to stop at yellow traffic lights before they turn red. Such a golfer is usually correct, but irritates companions by providing unneeded and unwanted rule citations.

At the opposite extreme are players who consistently fail to play by the rules (the same folks who run stop signs daily) and players who play as if they were unaware of basic golfing etiquette (the folks who neglect their turn signals). Rules-deficient golfers can become a problem, especially in competitive play. They might under-report their strokes, improve a lie, or fail to call penalty strokes on themselves.

Changing the situation with the rules-obsessed player can be relatively easy. An initial comment on the first tee can establish how serious this game will be. You might say, "We're all playing for fun today, so score-keeping can be as flexible as each of us wants it to be," or, "We can all take a mulligan on the front and back nine."

If the game is serious, then dealing with players who take liberties with the rules can be more challenging, especially among friends. If the lax player is known to the group, a comment before play like "Today we are going to play by the book" may suffice.

Sometimes players make honest mistakes. So, saying something like "I thought you had two shots out of the rough" might be enough. Breaches of etiquette are usually caused by lack of knowledge and can often be fixed by a quick comment.

Of course, the ultimate way to change the situation is to stop inviting the person to play with you.

Playing with Better Golfers. You may become stressed when playing with much better golfers, feeling you must play to their standards. This can happen when playing in a Pro-Am tournament, with a professional golfer, or with the club professional.

In such cases, emphasize the coping strategy of *changing yourself.* Focus on the cause of your stress. Is it because the other golfer is better, or is it because you feel inadequate? If it is the latter, adjust your thinking to focus on what you can learn from the other golfer.

> ### *Reminder: Golf = Fun*
>
> *Matt was an invited guest at a Pro-Am tournament. One of his amateur playing partners confided that he was nervous playing with an expert like Matt. Matt chuckled, "I am here to have fun playing with you. I hope that your goal is to have fun playing with me!" This statement relieved the tension by focusing on the real goal of enjoying the game, not judging each other.*

Everyone makes swing errors and mechanical mistakes; the more skilled golfer just makes fewer of them. Try to identify the elements of the better player's game that you can duplicate, and then own for yourself.

When playing a more skilled person, focus on playing your game *at your comfort level.* Play the way you *can* play. Avoid comparing yourself with a better golfer, because this leads to must-thinking: attempting to play the way you think you **must** play. As we have said, letting your expectations exceed your skill level only leads to frustration, stress, and poor shots.

Here's a fine example of how to learn from a better golfer:

LeBron was asked to play in a best-ball tournament where he was paired with two excellent young college women golfers. They were better than LeBron in every aspect of the game. He felt pretty inadequate.

On the tenth green, LeBron noticed that both other players hit low chip shots with their lob wedges. Their shots went straight to the hole, rolled briefly, and stopped quickly. He asked how they executed this shot. They showed him how to play the ball back in his stance, shift his weight forward, and hit down and through the ball.

He decided to replace the lofted pitch shot he'd been hitting with his sand wedge to this more controlled shot. It took two weeks of practice, but within a month this shot helped him reduce his handicap by two strokes.

Playing a Golfer You Should Beat, But Don't. Competitive players occasionally find themselves playing someone they should beat but don't. You and the other golfer may be evenly matched, yet that person consistently beats you. For example, your challenger may be someone who hits poorly but putts well, and thus edges you out by a shot or two.

1. **Try changing yourself by examining your game.** If your basic golf stroke is holding you back, take time to identify the elements you need to improve. Use the on-course shot analysis we recommend in Chapter 10. Identify your strengths and one or two shots you need to improve, and then work on them. You might even rethink your practice routine. As we pointed out in Chapter 12, a poorly thought-

out practice plan can't help your game, no matter how many shot-improvement lessons you take. You might also look at your course-management style. Are you making great shots, but ones that position you so you are forced to make plays outside your comfort zone? If so, rethink how you play.

2. **Take stock of your "hot buttons."** Which one does this person push? Are they doing it deliberately, trying to psych you out? Or are they innocent, and you are just generating your own stress?

    If you believe your companion is trying to psych you out, then call them on it. "I know you outdrove me on the past three holes, but look at the score. Let's see if you can out-putt me." Other alternatives: "Wow, you're hitting it great. Too bad the ball isn't finding the hole," or, "It's too bad that you are playing much better than you are scoring." These remarks do not insult your opponent, but they sure keep the competitive element alive in his or her mind!

    For some, playing with better players is stressful. To erase the tension, stress, and anxiety you may unconsciously associate with these individuals, suggest that the two of you play friendly practice rounds so you get used to playing that person under minimum tension. Frequency breeds familiarity, and this will increase your comfort level when playing with these stronger golfers.

    Other personal hot buttons include competitiveness, stubbornness, temper, a sense of failure, or a feeling that you do not measure up. The list is long. *Step one is to recognize the feeling and its source.* When you are honest with your mental and mechanical self-appraisal by identifying the barriers to your success, you have a greater chance of overcoming them.

Stressful Holes

Almost every course has a hole that is personally challenging. These can range from holes lined with narrow fairways surrounded by water to bunkers waiting to eat the ball to tricky turtle-shell greens that shed balls. Some golfers call these their "omen hole" or "jinxed hole."

These holes may change from month to month or year to year. The stressful holes are ones we face frequently and cause us anxiety. Once again, you can either change the situation or change yourself.

To change the situation, play the hole differently. If the tee shot gives you trouble, use a different club to drive. If the green is the problem, hit to another part of it, no matter where the hole is located.

To change yourself, you can change your reaction to the hole by playing it many times in a row. Pick a time when you will not interfere with other golfers, and play the hole six or eight times. This will help change your thinking from "must do well on this hole" to "can do well on this hole."

An example: Dawn often played a short 140-yard par-three hole with a pond between the tee and the green. For the past three rounds she had disasters hitting across it. Dawn could hit a 140-yard shot with a 7-iron a million times without problem, but she always started thinking about that evil pond as soon as she stepped off the previous green. This pattern started the day she slapped four balls into the water before hitting the green.

So Dawn took a two-step approach to changing herself and her thinking patterns. First, during warm-ups before playing, she went to the practice range and imagined the hole. She hit eight shots 140 yards while imagining the pond between her and where she wanted the ball to go. She also disciplined herself to follow her pre-shot routine on the tee.

The more she focused on her swing thoughts, feel, and body movement, the less time she had to think about the water. Finally, she learned to look at her target—the flag—and not the water. As she thought less about the water, the more successful she became.

Stressful Shots

Stressful shots pester people at every golfing level from *beginner*s to *experts*. We all have situations on the course that get our hearts racing a little faster.

For some, it might be a specific shot with a specific club. For others, it might be an intimidating distance to conquer. Some folks wince at the idea of hitting out of a bunker and others cringe when faced with a long approach shot on a par-five hole.

Here are some stressful shots, and our suggestions for dealing with them.

1. **Shots that get under your skin.** To change the situation, try playing away from conditions that require uncomfortable shots. This includes changing your course management strategy.

   Using this technique, take care to hit to positions where you can make your more comfortable shot. You might lay up to a point where you are comfortable hitting to the green.

   Our friend Tailor has a booming drive and gets a thrill from smacking his long irons 200 yards. Following his second shot on par-five holes, he usually lies less than 20 yards from the green. Unfortunately, he does not have a reliable 20-yard shot, and frequently miss-hits them. Not surprisingly, we noticed that Tailor was often tense when facing these short shots. We suggested that he play his second shot with a club that would leave him at a comfortable 110 yards away. Then, he could hit to the green with a full swing, a shot he could make all of the time. By playing to this go-to shot, Tailor was able to alleviate his stress level, and in turn reduce the number of bogies on these holes.

2. **Your club suddenly turns on you like a snake.** Our primary advice here is to hit the shot with the club that is easiest for you. This is another example of *Must vs. Can* thinking. Change your thinking from belief that you **must** hit a certain club, and select a club you **can** use comfortably. If the driver starts giving you trouble, use a three wood or rescue club.

   Fred's driver was suddenly possessed by a slice serpent. Most of his drives began seeking trees and bushes to the right of the fairway. After six holes of stress-building frustration, he put the driver away and switched to the 3-wood. This more forgiving club cost him 15 yards in distance, but left him with more reasonable second shots and a more relaxed swing.

3. **Your lack of skill makes too many shots stressful.** If inexperience and lack of skill are a problem, your first fix is to get lessons from a professional teacher and then to practice the shots. Our games will give you the practice experience. Once you gain the basic foundation for a shot, giving yourself the opportunity to play it many times on the course will build your confidence.

    Several games in the *On the Course* booklet such as *Limit* or *Round Robin* require you to play with a limited number of clubs for a round. Choose your problem clubs for these games so you will become comfortable with them.

4. **Your Memory of Stressful Shots Is Killing Your Confidence.** The toughest thing to overcome is memory—especially unhappy memories of that three putt, or skulled chip, or drive that duck-hooked into the jungle where you waded through snake-infested poison ivy to retrieve it.

    It is human nature to review your mistakes and undervalue your successes. (This is our survival instinct at work, making us focus on where we experienced danger, so we won't go there again.) The trick here is to change your thinking. Recall situations where you hit a shot well. Less-skilled players, especially, dwell too much on mistakes. Whenever the pressure of miss-hits threatens to ruin your game, focus on your successful shots in the past.

Stressful Environments

If something makes you uncomfortable with the playing environment, it can be very stressful. Factors include participating in a championship, waiting for a slow-playing group ahead of you to move on, playing competitively for money, lousy weather, or any condition that does not directly involve people, shots, or holes.

So, how to deal with stressful environments?

1. **Tournament Stress.** Matt and Dean were partners in a challenging Pro-Pro tournament. They were determined to win, since their opponents had beaten them the last time they played. Tournament stress bit them, and they started off poorly on the first two holes. But instead of becoming discouraged, they made a simple pact that promoted a different attitude: "We will not suck!" They sealed this agreement with a high-five.

   > No one watching cares what you do [on the first tee]. Golfers are too worried about what other people will think of them. No one cares. The other people are busy worrying about their own first shot.
   >
   > —Butch Harmon

   They then proceeded to play every shot with the attitude that they would never miss a shot or a putt. They started to the next hole two over par, but proceeded to play nine under for the remaining holes and tie for first place—beating their opponents.

2. **First-tee jitters.** This is one of the most common environmental stressors. We tend to get physically tight, and typically there is a group of strangers standing around watching. You can change this in several ways:

   - **Loosen up on the range before the round.** When you make the last four or five shots practice shots, imagine that you are on the first tee. Make sure the last shot is a good one.

   - **Focus on your pre-shot routine and stay focused on your key swing thoughts.** Remind yourself that the shot off the first tee is only one shot for the day. Or, imagine that you are on the second tee with no one else around.

   - **Change the emotional situation on the first tee.** Usually, on the first tee, people are all too serious. Joke with your playing partners or onlookers to relieve the tension. Do something neutral that will divert your attention from the shot, but not distract other players, such as cleaning a club or selecting a tee.

Matt had a clever way of dealing with a student who had first-tee jitters when playing social golf with her friends. This initial shot affected her so much that she felt it better not to play at all than face the tension of that first shot!

Matt gave her a simple suggestion to change the situation: "Don't hit off the first tee! Drop a ball in the fairway and play from there." She exclaimed, "But is that legal?" Matt assured her: "You're playing for fun, not competing in a tournament, so rules can be waived." Matt helped her cope by showing how to change the situation to be less demanding.

3. **Dispel Your Demons.** Your attitude toward the playing environment is something you can control. Here's an example:

   One hole on a difficult course was an extremely tough 470-yard par-four that made "demons" creep into Terry's thoughts. There was an out-of-bounds very close to the right. There were trees to the left,

   > Why am I using a new putter? Because the old one did not float too well.
   >
   > —Craig Stadler

   and if Terry bailed out to the left, he most likely would make a bogey. To eradicate the demons, Terry did not hit the tee shot until he was comfortable with the situation. His routine took a little longer. He made a few additional practice swings and stayed away from the ball until he was comfortable. He squashed the demons with a perfect drive to the right center of the fairway.

   The additional time to relax and focus on his successful pre-shot routine helped Terry succeed where success had been infrequent. Focusing on the pre-shot routine encouraged confidence and commitment to the shot. Commitment is 90% of success.

4. **The Older I Get, the Better I Was.** As we age, we lose some flexibility, balance, and strength. Highly competent players tend to recall what they once were capable of, instead of what they actually can do today. Their declining game leads to frustration. This is the "Older I get, the better I was" syndrome.

This can be disappointing as scores start to rise. Here it is important to adjust your thinking so that your game keeps pace with your expectations, and your expectations match your life situation. This is one of the hardest adjustments better golfers have to make as they age.

Try playing from different tees. If you were used to playing from championship blue tees, move to the white ones or the red ones. We are not suggesting that you stop challenging yourself! We are simply encouraging you to play the game you can play when the chips are on the line. You'll enjoy it more.

Another adaptation as you age is to adjust your expectations for how far you can hit the ball. Try one of the shot inventories in Chapter 9. It may be that instead of hitting your 7-iron 150 yards, you should drop down to your 6-iron.

As a seasoned golfer, one advantage you have over most other players is your short game. If length off the tee is an issue, then focus on approach shots, chipping, pitching, and putting.

Keep in mind that in many individual sports, such as track and field, the Senior Golf Tour, and horse racing, adjustments are made for older players. Remember, our goal in golf is to have fun. For some this comes from the game itself, for others it comes from socializing, still others gain their pleasure from the competition.

Don't let your pride get in the way of enjoying the game!

Frustration and Anger

Think about a beautiful day when you went out to play a round with friends. Your hopes were high for an exceptional round. This was not just wishful thinking—the last time, you had your best score ever. As you approached the first tee, you knew that your golf game had reached a new level.

The wheels came off. The driver went berserk, your irons turned into lead sticks, and your putter took a holiday to Outer Mongolia. By the fourth hole, you felt volcanic. You hooked a short drive into the forest and almost broke your driver slamming it back into the bag.

Many of us know the satisfying whoop-whoop-whoop of a well-thrown club followed by the sheepish shuffle of shame while we shamble off to retrieve it! This is the frequent reaction to the frustration of having hit a terrible shot.

While ignoring an errant ball may be the "adult" thing to do, it is difficult. It is liberating to know that frustration is allowed on the course. You just have to recognize it and deal with it before it destroys your game and upsets your companions.

Frustration-Aggression

A major psychological theory that explains the inner turmoil you feel is the *frustration-aggression hypothesis*.

Frustration occurs when you are blocked from reaching an important goal, like a good shot or score. The natural consequence of frustration in people is aggression.

A bad shot is frustrating. If you are stressed this frustration generates anger. This anger must be directed at something, so we direct it at the club, the ball, the bag, or ourselves.

Some years ago, professional golfer Woody Austin missed a relatively easy putt at a tournament in Texas. Austin had a pretty fast trigger, and took out his frustration on himself and the putter by hitting himself over the head with the club and bending it. He had to finish the round without the putter, since it was altered during the course of play. Using it would have disqualified him!

> Like all other pleasures immoderately enjoyed, the excesses of hope must be expiated by pain; and expectations improperly indulged must end in disappointment.
>
> —Samuel Johnson

Many of us have experienced the desire to rampage after a series of disappointing shots, especially when they are ones we know we can make. Some of us have given in to this frustration-driven emotion. Since this is so common, we decided to identify how this occurs for golfers.

Frustration Trigger: Expectations

In Chapter 10, we discussed expectations in the context of learning and practicing golf. Now we would like to discuss expectations in terms of how they can both improve and harm your golf game. *Remember that your expectation is your belief about what you should be able to accomplish.* When playing golf you have a belief (expectation) about how well you will hit a shot or how your score will turn out.

When your expectations are met (or exceeded), you feel happy, even jubilant. No one really expects to get a hole-in-one, so when it happens, your expectations are exceeded. The result is euphoria and perhaps a hefty drink tab.

But golfing frustration begins when your expectations are not met about your score, your last shot, or yourself. We typically see this with *beginners* who do not have the experience to understand how complex the golf swing is. It looks so simple! Then they get out on the course with expectations that far exceed their skill. In this case, their golfing expectations are truly the triumph of hope over experience.

As your swings become more consistent and predictable, your expectations and performance are more likely to be in balance. This does not mean that frustration ceases as you get better! As you get better, your golfing goals tend to rise.

Look at great professional golfers. Their goals are stratospheric, compared to the weekend player's. Yet, as the Woody Austin example points out, they lose their cool just like we do.

Frustration Trigger: When Your Golfing Skills Don't Live Up to Your Ambitions

This major outburst trigger often afflicts once-a-month players who expect to get expert scores. There are two fixes. You can either lower your expectations or raise your skills.

First, honestly assess your playing level. If you play once or twice a year, don't practice, and your last lesson was with hickory-shafted clubs and feather-filled balls (we're talking 1700s here), then it is only wishful thinking for you to play like an expert. Your goal should be to learn to play for the fun of being outdoors and companionship. Stop fretting about hitting the ball flawlessly, adjust your ambitions, and enjoy the game.

The other fix for a skill/ambition mismatch is to improve your game. Review Chapters 10 and 11, take lessons, practice efficiently, and work through some of our games.

Calm Players

The calm player has learned that errant balls are part of the game. Of course they are disappointed with a poor shot, but they don't dwell on them. Here are some of their strategies:

- Acknowledge the bad shot and move on to the next one. (Calm players have disciplined themselves to look ahead, not back.)
- Focus on the good shots while acknowledging the bad ones. (Calm players have learned how to balance annoyance at poor shots with pleasure over the good ones.)
- Focus on the details of the pre-shot routine for the next stroke.
- Practice physical and emotional relaxation techniques. (Some players use yoga, meditation, or other techniques to relax and clear their minds.)
- Know how to vent your frustration; then turn and prepare for the next shot.
- Develop and practice a poor-shot cool-off routine.
- Bite a tee, eat a piece of fruit, or chew a fresh piece of gum as a trigger to remind yourself to relax.

Keeping Your Perspective

Our friend Terry is a competitive mid-90s golfer. He was paired with an expert partner at a moderately demanding 18-hole course in South Carolina. Terry's game started poorly and fell apart as he tried to get out of the same greenside bunker three times. In frustration, he threw his sand wedge at his bag. His playing companion, an elegant expert golfer from Argentina, gently placed his hand on Terry's shoulder and said, "My friend, you don't play golf well enough to get so angry."

Terry was given a key lesson. He had placed too much importance on playing perfectly, and not enough on the joy of playing with and learning from his companion.

Lee Trevino is reported to have said, "Show me someone who gets angry once in a while, and I will show you someone with a killer instinct. Show me a guy walking down the fairway smiling and I'll show you a loser." Intensity, focus, and competitiveness are all necessary for winning at tournament golf. But in extremes, these emotions can disable you, your game, and your companions when playing social golf. Competitiveness is okay, even expected. But for golfers playing in friendly games, the aggressive killer attitude is inappropriate.

In the end, unlike jousting, golf is a friendly game—a game to be played with joy. When you find yourself getting discouraged, remember what President Woodrow Wilson said: "Golf is an ineffectual attempt to put an elusive ball into an obscure hole with implements ill-adapted to the purpose."

See You on the Course!

In this book, we have shown you:

- How to identify the swing mechanics you should work on to enhance your game.
- How to incorporate the techniques you want to learn by developing an efficient, personalized practice routine.
- Ways to gain insight into how you can control the emotional elements of your game.
- Dozens of swing-improvement games you can play either alone or with friends.

As the great sportswriter Grantland Rice observed, "Golf is 20% mechanics and technique. The other 80% is philosophy, humor, tragedy, romance, melodrama, companionship, camaraderie, cussedness, and conversation."

See you on the course—for fun!

Appendix

\	PUTTING CIRCLE											
\	H = Hit X = Miss-hit				L = Left R = Right				S = Short Lo = Long			
Feet from pin	First Series				Second Series				Third Series			
^	Ball				Ball				Ball			
^	1	2	3	4	1	2	3	4	1	2	3	4
5'												
10'												
15'												
20'												
25'												

Notes and comments

CHIPPING CIRCLE — Club Used

H = Hit
X = Miss-hit

L = Left
R = Right

S = Short
Lo = Long

Yards from pin	First Series Ball				Second Series Ball				Third Series Ball			
	1	2	3	4	1	2	3	4	1	2	3	4
5												
10												
15												
20												
25												

Notes and comments

PITCHING—Club Used

| H = Hit | L = Left | S = Short |
| X = Miss-hit | R = Right | Lo = Long |

Yards from pin	First Series — Ball				Second Series — Ball				Third Series — Ball			
	1	2	3	4	1	2	3	4	1	2	3	4
10												
15												
25												
30												
50												

Notes and comments

APPENDIX

BUNKER EVALUATION — Club Used

H = Hit
X = Miss-hit

L = Left
R = Right

S = Short
Lo = Long

Yards from pin	First Series Ball				Second Series Ball				Third Series Ball			
	1	2	3	4	1	2	3	4	1	2	3	4
5												
10												
15												
20												
25												

Notes and comments

LONG CHIP—Club Used

H = Hit / X = Miss-hit			L = Left / R = Right				S = Short / Lo = Long
Yards to Target	Ball						Comment
	1	2	3	4	5	6	
25							
50							
75							
100							

LONG CHIP—Club Used

H = Hit / X = Miss-hit			L = Left / R = Right				S = Short / Lo = Long
Yards to Target	Ball						Comment
	1	2	3	4	5	6	
25							
50							
75							
100							

FULL SWING SCORING SHEET

Club	Club used	|1|2|3|4|5|6|7|8|9|10| Distance	Comment

Club	Club used	1	2	3	4	5	6	7	8	9	10	Comment
Lob Wedge												
Sand Wedge												
Gap Wedge												
Pitching Wedge												
9-iron												
8-iron												
7-iron												
6-iron												
5-iron												
4-iron												
3-iron												
2-iron												
7-wood												
5-wood												
3-wood												
Driver												

FULL SWING SCORING SHEET

Club	Club used	____ Distance ____										Comment
		1	2	3	4	5	6	7	8	9	10	
Lob Wedge												
Sand Wedge												
Gap Wedge												
Pitching Wedge												
9-iron												
8-iron												
7-iron												
6-iron												
5-iron												
4-iron												
3-iron												
2-iron												
7-wood												
5-wood												
3-wood												
Driver												

GOAL PLANNING GUIDE

GOAL (What I want to achieve)

BENEFITS (What I will get from achieving this goal)

1.	
2.	

HOW WILL I GET THERE? (Steps to achieve this goal)

	Action Steps	Target Dates
1.		
2.		
3.		
4.		

WHAT DO I NEED TO GET THERE? (Time, Material, Money, Information)

Time	
Material	
Money	
Information	

POSSIBLE OBSTACLES (What could interfere with achieving this goal)

1.	
2.	

POSSIBLE SOLUTIONS TO OBSTACLES (Ways to get around obstacles)

1.	
2.	

HOW CAN I TRACK MY PROGRESS? (How will I know I am reaching this goal?)

1.	
2.	

WHO WILL HELP ME TRACK MY PROGRESS?

1.	
2.	

IS THIS GOAL WORTH THE TIME, EFFORT, MONEY, AND TRAINING?
YES: _____ **NO:** _____ **YES, BUT LATER:** _____

GOAL PLANNING GUIDE

GOAL (What I want to achieve)

BENEFITS (What I will get from achieving this goal)

1.	
2.	

HOW WILL I GET THERE? (Steps to achieve this goal)

	Action Steps	**Target Dates**
1.		
2.		
3.		
4.		

WHAT DO I NEED TO GET THERE? (Time, Material, Money, Information)

Time	
Material	
Money	
Information	

POSSIBLE OBSTACLES (What could interfere with achieving this goal)

1.	
2.	

POSSIBLE SOLUTIONS TO OBSTACLES (Ways to get around obstacles)

1.	
2.	

HOW CAN I TRACK MY PROGRESS? (How will I know I am reaching this goal?)

1.	
2.	

WHO WILL HELP ME TRACK MY PROGRESS?

1.	
2.	

IS THIS GOAL WORTH THE TIME, EFFORT, MONEY, AND TRAINING?

YES: _____ NO: _____ YES, BUT LATER: _____

Glossary

Approach shot: a shot from the fairway where the person takes a full swing with the goal of landing the ball on a specific target, usually the green.

Birdie: scoring 1 under par on a golf hole, a very good score. (Par, remember, is the expected number of strokes it should take an expert golfer to complete a hole.)

Bunker: a hazard consisting of a prepared area of ground, often a hollow, from which turf or soil has been removed and replaced with sand or the like.

Handicap: numerical representation of a golfer's playing ability; the lower a handicap, the better the golfer.

Lie: Location of the ball at rest—where it "lies."

Lofted club—Lofted refers to the angle of a club's face. A "lofted" club "lofts" the ball into the air quickly.

Par: is the expected number of strokes an expert would take to complete a hole.

Pitch: a stroke where you do not take a full swing and the ball flies more than it rolls. The goal is to get the ball close to the hole.

Pitch Mark: The depression made in the putting surface by a ball when it lands on the green.

Practicing: an activity in which you actively repeat some skill with the goal of either improving or maintaining it.

Putt: a stroke where the ball stays on the ground with the goal of getting it into the hole.

Rollout: distance a ball rolls after it hits the green.

Scratch Golfer: a excellent golfer having a handicap of 0 or less (average score for a round is par or better).

Tee shot: any shot made from the tee box. The goal is to either advance the ball down the fairway or, for par-three holes, hit the green.